*This book is dedicated
to Susan,
who aided me in countless ways.*

LEADERSHIP GAMES

Stephen S. Kaagan

Experiential Learning for
Organizational Development

SAGE Publications
International Educational and Professional Publisher
Thousand Oaks London New Delhi

For information:

SAGE Publications, Inc.
2455 Teller Road
Thousand Oaks, California 91320
E-mail: order@sagepub.com

SAGE Publications Ltd.
6 Bonhill Street
London EC2A 4PU
United Kingdom

SAGE Publications India Pvt. Ltd.
M-32 Market
Greater Kailash I
New Delhi 110 048 India

Printed in the United States of America

Library of Congress Cataloging-in-Publication Data

Kaagan, Stephen S.
    Leadership games: Experiential learning for organizational
development / by Stephen S. Kaagan.
        p.   cm.
    Includes bibliographical references
        ISBN 0-7619-1721-7 (pbk.: acid-free paper)
        1. Leadership. 2. Management games. 3. Experiential learning.
    I. Title
    HD57.7 .K3 1998
    658.4'07124—ddc21   98-25396

This book is printed on acid-free paper.

99 00 01 02 03 04 05 7 6 5 4 3 2

Acquiring Editor:	Marquita Flemming
Editorial Assistant:	Mary Ann Vail
Production Editor:	Denise Santoyo
Editorial Assistant:	Stephanie Allen
Typesetter/Designer:	Lynn Miyata
Illustrator:	David G. Kaagan

LEADERSHIP GAMES

SOUTHAMPTON INSTITUTE

Contents

Prologue

Ten upper-level managers gather on an ocean front dock in Penobscot Bay, Maine. They are participants in a professional development program sponsored by their company, the aim of which is to enhance communication and coordination among top management. Soon they will embark on an ocean journey in a 30-foot, ketch-rigged sailing craft that resembles a bathtub, or, to be more generous, a lifeboat from the *Titanic*. It has two small sails and no motor—and no on-board bathroom facilities. The boat itself bobs in the gentle swells of the harbor in front of the participants' wary eyes. All the gear and food that they will need for their several days together in tight quarters is at their feet on the dock.

An instructor joins them, introduces himself, and asks them quietly if they wouldn't mind counting off, 1 to 10. "For safety purpose mostly," he says. After all have done so, the instructor inquires as to who was number one. Following a short pause, a person off to the side answers, "It was me." "Good," says the instructor, "you'll be the captain." "Hunh?" says the startled participant, caught a bit off guard, "I don't even know how to sail." The instructor barely pauses to reply, "It's OK, you'll learn, I'll help. Now, who was number two?"

There is much useful perspective to be drawn from this vignette. First, the whole sequence is counterintuitive in terms of the way most people think about learning. The traditional sequence is that instruction precedes practice. Right? But maybe not; it could be the other way round. A second interesting piece is the relationship among instructor, learners, and the "classroom." Deftly, the instructor allows the challenges that inhere in the context—ocean, harbor swells, boat, sails, a dock full of gear and provisions—to take hold of the participants, to form for them the base of their potential engagement with the task at hand.

Third, the instructor arrives at and assigns key responsibilities in a random manner, by lot. In so doing, he simultaneously proffers the mantle of leadership on all. This would have to be the case if such important assignments could be distributed to anyone at will. Fourth, the attention of those assigned the top jobs is riveted as fantasies regarding what they are about to do and where they are about to go dance in front of their eyes. Very important for learning that the learners pay attention, right? In this instance, all might agree that the instructor succeeds not only in getting the learners' attention but also in tapping into a reservoir of motivation for learning. Apprehension about the unknown, as long as its debilitating effects can be blunted, is a powerful motivator.

All that unfolds on the dock may be no more than a beginning; but in a fundamental sense, it is a most satisfactory beginning. It provides a solid platform for potential learning, without which there can be no learning at all. This book, like the vignette on the dock, is about building a fit platform for leadership learning. It describes constructed experiences that promote learning and shows how to use these experiences to overcome difficult organizational challenges.

Introduction

It is the recipient who communicates. The so-called communicator, the person who emits the communication, does not communicate. He utters. Unless there is someone who hears, there is no communication. There is only noise (Drucker, 1974, p. 483).

Tough challenges await those who seek to lead modern organizations. Four of the toughest for leaders and those who work with them are

- risking innovation,
- fostering collaboration,
- managing conflict, and
- using diversity.

This book is about how to develop the capacity of leaders in any field of endeavor to overcome these challenges on behalf of the organizational missions they serve. At its heart, it is about becoming familiar with, choosing, and using much simpler, yet more powerful, instruments for leadership development than have been employed to date. It is a primer in a field that may well have become saturated with cumbersome and costly treatments that provide only modest benefits for the people they were designed to serve.

For you, the reader, this book is an unique opportunity to enhance your own capability and the capabilities of those you seek to influence. It invites you to consider carefully the present state of the art of leadership development. But it offers considerably more than a discussion of where things are on this important front. It also presents a set of exercises that you can adapt to fulfill legitimate organizational ends in a manner that fits your own aims, philosophy, and style. If you use what is here, you will both broaden your repertoire and sharpen your skills as a teacher of leadership. After all, supervising other people entails more than anything else teaching leadership.

A number of noted contemporary analysts—Lee Bolman and Terrance Deal (1991, 1994), Kenneth and Miriam Clark (1994), Ronald Heifitz (1994)—argue that leadership development efforts, if they are ever to have greater effect, must become much more experiential and much less didactic. In its simplest form, what these experts are calling for is less lecturing about the craft. They are asking instead that learners be granted more opportunity to experience situations, problems, and challenges. Then, through well-facilitated discussions and directed reading and writing about their experiences, leaders in the making can expand their portfolio of enlightened leadership practices. Practices learned this way, it is argued, would have a greater hold on minds, a more pronounced effect on the way these leaders work, and a more significant influence on their workplaces.

On their face, the arguments of these commentators make sense. The underlying rationale is indisputable: People adopt new approaches more quickly if they are encouraged to revise their ideas about how to do things through intense and directed examination of what they have been doing. This is what is meant by reflection. Interestingly, a wide range of experiences can serve well as platforms for reflection, including ones drawn from people's workplace as well as constructed experiences such as simulations or exercises. The key is whether any given experience contains potentially relevant material for learning.

Yet the simple idea of grounding leadership learning in experience contrasts with the mode that continues to dominate today. The standard representation is large numbers of listeners sitting at rows of tables leaning on their elbows for support as they are provided a rendition of new approaches to leadership and their potential applicability in the workplace. The listeners are left to work through in their own heads exactly what the lessons are, which ones to apply, and how to apply them within their own organization.

Common sense tells us that we learn more through doing and reflecting on doing than through listening, absorbing, and reframing. This is especially true of a topic such as leadership that is so richly personal, social, and political. Through a doing and reflecting sequence, the learner wrestles with the dynamics of change and development in the context of recent behavior and interactions with colleagues.

The here-and-now of experience, if well mediated by an effective facilitator, can provide a demanding environment in which learning can be deeper, more consequential, and more enduring. Experience is real and its effects are immediate. It happened. It must somehow be reckoned with. Although apprehended differently by different people, experience itself warrants that concepts put forth connect in some way with participants' observations of what happened within the experience.

In the listening, absorbing, reframing sequence—what some call "sitting and gitting,"—the learner can languish in the realm of ideas. There is not the discomfort that emerges as a result of the presence of overpowering evidence drawn from the learner's recent behavior. It is this very discomfort that can provoke altered perspective and promote ways of doing things differently in the future, much more so than a detached idea can.

Although the power of an idea might overtake the thoughts of the listener, thinking good ideas about leadership does not necessarily result in doing good leadership. For the listener, it is just too easy to speculate, whether seriously or casually, on what might be desirable to do, and then in fact do nothing. The frequently observed sequence is that a person fits what he or she has heard to his or her way of thinking, convincing himself or herself that he or she is already really doing what the speaker asserts is valuable, and decides to go on pretty much as before.

This process—listening, absorbing, rationalizing, and reverting to (in lieu of revamping) the status quo—accurately describes a large part of the leadership development enterprise as presently practiced. At ground level, here is how it works: Selected representatives of a firm go off to a highly touted and highly priced leadership development conference. Upon returning, they talk in animated tones and laudatory terms about what they heard, certain that the perspectives provided will cause them to reshape how they go about fundamental aspects of their work together. Not long after, the ideas drawn from the conference begin to command less discussion; the materials they brought back with them start to disappear under papers reflecting competing priorities; and the enthusiasm of the participants, so strong in the wake of the presentation, gradually fades. Even though some of the terminology remains in their weekly meeting rhetoric, very little else is different from the way it was before.

There is, among other things, significantly less inherent individual accountability in the more didactic forms of leadership development. Rationalizing ideas, privately apprehended as a listener in a large room, is a path of least resistance. It is much easier than rationalizing actions that were demonstrated in the open in front of a small group of one's peers.

My own experience may be illustrative here. Once, in doing an exercise that emphasized the imperative of planners and implementers working in collaboration rather than in isolation, one of the designated planners slammed the door in the face of an implementer who had come politely seeking to understand what the planners were up to. In the discussion that followed the activity, the planner, who was in real life the ranking executive in the group, valiantly asserted a firm and enduring commitment to collaboration. There was, however, no way she could escape the profoundly noncollaborative move she had made moments ago. It warranted attention and received ample discussion in spite of her attempts to downplay it. This all made for some welcome, or unwelcome, accountability, depending on whose shoes you wore.

Regardless of how compelling the case for experiential leadership development is, it has yet to take hold in many quarters. An emerging consensus among experts on the matter has not eased the way to realizing its proper place. As is true in most human endeavors, making something happen is much harder than making a case for it to happen. Ironically, the gap between theory and practice in leadership development is as great as that which exists in leadership itself. Insistent exhortations about good (read collaborative) leadership practices have had only marginal effect on workplace behavior. Urgings about good (read experienced-based) leadership development have similarly had limited effect. Most of what passes for leadership development in the public and private sectors is still heavily didactic, despite convincing arguments to the contrary.

The failure to make the desired shift to more experiential approaches is not just the result of normal implementation snags. Interestingly, there is at present no shortage of materials and basic know-how about experiential leadership development techniques. Any willing and able human resource specialist can locate enough resources to move forward with dispatch. Published case studies, guided management simulations and games, and formulas for apprenticeships and internships as well as public and community service opportunities have all been available in multiple sectors for several decades. The current literature on leadership development also provides ample treatment of all the above at both theoretical and practical levels. A cursory visit to the leadership and management section of a decent-sized bookstore will confirm this point.

So what are the hang-ups, the hold-ups, the hitches? They are threefold:

- Methods of teaching transform slowly, more slowly, in fact, than any art or technology, regardless of the sector to which they are being applied.

- Experiential teaching approaches are not easily packaged, and therefore pose problems for the provider who knows that volume distribution and easy repetition are the routes to profitability.

- The desire of service providers for profits, spurred by the indiscriminate appetite of clients with genuine needs, has all but relegated experiential forms of leadership development to the shelf featuring the "high-priced spreads."

These three factors have served to inhibit the move of experiential methods into the mainstream of leadership development practices. This book is an attempt to set all three aside and pave the way for the more regular and easy use of experiential methods.

A short anecdote illuminates the dynamics of the first inhibitor, that teaching methods shift slowly. A large and well-respected educational organization asked me a few years ago to help shape its national leadership conference into a more experiential event. In the words of one of the top staff, the organization's leaders wanted to be truer to their own advocacy for more active forms of learning. As the time of the event approached, however, my clients decided to go back to their traditional format, involving keynote speakers and panels on daises. The proposed experiential approaches were confined to a small corner of the agenda for a limited few who were willing to go out of their way to gain access to them.

At root, the sponsors of the event were afraid that they would not be able to control the flow of discussion in the experiential sessions as much as they could in the didactic presentations. They were also concerned that their constituents might be put off by a format that demanded more engagement from them as participants. The attendees had, after all, paid their money and should not be disrupted from getting exactly what they had been getting without interruption for the past several decades— talking heads. A philosophical—and even a financial—commitment to more active forms of learning was not enough to overtake a set of enduring commitments to well-worn methods.

Experiential teaching, however, is not just a frequent victim of deep allegiances to the way things have always been done. In some respects it is its own worst enemy, its greatest weaknesses stemming from its greatest strength. The activities associated with experiential teaching engage, at times even rivet, the attention of participants. Simulations, games, exercises, problem-solving initiatives gain a quick and firm hold on those who join in. They almost inevitably afford people a "good ride." Yet, however engaging the activities, they can be egregiously devoid of new ideas, notoriously incapable of engendering new ideas, and, all in all, impotent at provoking fundamentally different ways of doing business.

The best of the new thinking about leadership has yet to gain a firm foothold in the experiences generally provided to participants. Facilitators often fail to weave new ideas into the critical discussions that follow an experience. Instead, they tend to rehash what happened in an activity and leave it at that. As long as this represents the net yield of debriefs, then the growth of experiential leadership development will remain stunted.

Just as ideas can easily remain detached from experience, experience can easily remain detached from ideas. Beyond the sidelining of new thinking about leadership, most experiential leadership development efforts have also, to their great detriment, kept essential organizational development objectives to the side. Effective links are rarely made between what participants are experiencing in an exercise and the larger challenges confronting organizations.

What is needed instead is real clarity about how experiential approaches can be targeted to fulfill aims integral to the successful functioning of organizations. Experiential approaches cannot continue to dangle somewhat aimlessly in a nether world, on the one extreme, detached from the larger problems of work in organizations, or on the other, tightly tied to narrow realms of technical knowledge with little potential for application in broader contexts.

The second point, that experiential methods do not lend themselves to a volume business and to easy repetitions, should be self-evident. Experiences that bear the earmarks of solid preparation and sound debriefing cannot just be "cranked out" on a "take it and use it" basis. As the chapters that follow demonstrate, thoughtfulness and discretion are necessary. Like good cooking, sound experiential leadership development requires careful preparation and artful execution, with the facilitator-cook standing ready to deal on the spot with unexpected developments as the ingredients are combined and the heat is applied.

Never, for example, was I more speechless than when I was running a simple group problem-solving exercise in a sylvan setting for a group of educators. After the exercise, I asked the participants to sit down on the lawn so we could discuss what had just happened in the activity. One of the participants blurted out, "I don't do grass." I knew instantaneously that she was not making a pun, even though some of her peers tried to twist it into one for humor's sake. As it turned out, she had spent her entire life in inner-city settings and was dead serious about not wanting to sit on the grass. After alighting on the obvious alternative of inviting her to stand, I took a moment to appreciate a truth that every facilitator is wont to forget: All learners have different starting places when it comes to discomfort and related learning thresholds. Everything is indeed contextual, and adaptation to context is integral to the workings of experiential leadership development in all its forms.

The third constraint on the expansion of experiential approaches is artificially induced high cost. Because of the effort and sophistication involved in designing and doing solid experiential leadership development, the prevailing assumption in the marketplace is that a lot of high-priced expertise and commitment of resource are required to do the job right. Although it is in many respects true that tailored experiences cost more, they do not need to command the price tags that have generally been attached to them.

It is as if the present leadership development industry has been segmented into two sectors, cheap and oversimplified versus expensive and overelaborate, with little in between that is worthy. Either one can go to Barnes & Noble and purchase a how-to manual on team development exercises for $15, or one can employ consultants of repute for $15,000. The absence of an effective middle ground is not satisfactory. It is possible, as this book demonstrates, to establish one, where tailored and well-guided programs can be had at much less than the top dollar they are now commanding, if the mind is applied and the will takes hold.

The present incapacitation that hampers the effective implementation of experiential leadership development, delivered at reasonable cost, represents a fit challenge. When enumerated and weighed, the three reasons underlying that incapacitation make up a set of needs whose fulfillment will dictate the pace and the extent of advancements in leadership development in the years ahead. The aim of this book is to meet these needs head on by providing a compelling and enticing invitation to organizational leaders to think and act differently when they go about the work of leadership development.

Put another way, the intent is to increase the intellectual capital available to individuals who could, if they chose to, improve the quality of leadership development opportunities offered to their coworkers. In this book, that capital takes the form of exemplary experiential exercises and, as important, the articulation of connections between the exercises and essential organizational objectives.

Considerable substantiation for the experiential approach as the preferred method of teaching already exists. The agenda here is to lay out a set of real possibilities and present them well enough to spur action by those concerned with the cost-effectiveness of leadership development programs.

True to its asserted teaching principles, the book is an invitation framed in experiential terms. It not only accepts the validity of the argument that leadership development efforts should be based more on participant experience, it lays out a path, both conceptual and practical, that will help the reader (read participant) make them that way.

Although much of the book is quite practical, the intention is not to produce a how-to piece. In addition to offering many concrete suggestions about how to do experiential leadership development, it also focuses on the why's and wherefore's that underpin the how's. There is ample discussion of teaching concepts, factors that motivate adult learners, broad organizational development purposes that specific exercises serve, and the pitfalls that might be encountered in earnest albeit unguided attempts to use experiential exercises for organizational development.

To fulfill its potential, experiential leadership development has to match the concerns of organizational leaders today. It also must stand up to the test that it is concerned with ingredients of leadership that are enduring. Four leadership ideas are the weight-bearing pillars of this book. They are *risking innovation, fostering collaboration, managing conflict,* and *using diversity.* Commentary of noted theorists and practitioners corroborate how integral these are to advanced and forward-looking thinking about leadership. *The Leaders of the Future* (1996), a recent collection of essays from the Drucker Foundation, makes the case well. It explores the perspectives of leading analysts and executives on the matter of critical aspects of leadership and principal themes in leadership development. The four ideas contained in this book receive focused attention from both those who frame ideas and those who execute them in today's organizations. In some greater depth, here is what they are about:

- Reasonable risk assumption and initiative taking involve pushing oneself and others with whom one is working to the creative edges of an undertaking so that it grows, spreads out, takes in new clients and customers, and serves them in new and more powerful ways. At the same time, whatever is done has to be done soberly. Rhetoric about the desirability of risk taking has outpaced reality in organizations, and the result is considerable cynicism in almost every quarter. Many in the middle and lower ranks of an enterprise hear repeatedly that they should take risks, innovate, show initiative. Yet when they do, more often than not they are knocked back. Prudently and predictably, they revert to behavior that is characterized by compliance with rules and regulations and pleasing the boss.
- The word *collaboration* is one of the most overused and misapplied terms in the work of today's organizations. Frequently, it heralds a leader's vague hope that a group of individuals might, when thrown together for a legitimate purpose, become a tightly knit and highly productive force within the organization. The hope is rarely realized. So-called teams disappoint more than they produce. Real collaboration, or teamwork, is a rarity. In its purest form, teamwork requires that a group of people act as one. Teams accomplish commonly held objectives. Members support each other's strengths and shore up each others' weaknesses. They are committed to holding each other mutually accountable for results. Successful teamwork is a product of artful *team building,* which takes time, energy, and savvy. It requires establishing team cohesiveness before teamwork on an assigned task actually gets underway. Cohesiveness develops from the application of sophisticated deliberation skills. Active, careful listening is critical, as is the adoption of strategies that make group discussions flow in the direction of desired results.
- Conflict is the one given likely to be present when two or more people get together to do something in an organization. Conflict is inevitable. Yet solid understanding that it is inevitable by all who are brought together to accomplish something is not inevitable. Most people operate within a realm of naïveté: They tend to think that what is in their head pretty much aligns with what is in other people's heads. That this is not the case is the root cause of conflict. Furthermore, it is also rarely the case that groups are well equipped to transform

conflict into an advantage for accomplishing an assigned task. Understanding the roots of group and organizational divisiveness is essential. Learning its positive uses and acquiring the means to deflect its negative effect are also essential. Promising approaches to resolving conflict depend on engaging with it.

• Using diversity refers to ways of achieving greater productivity in the context of challenges offered by racial, religious, ethnic, and gender differences. In many respects, it is an extension of the problem of managing conflict. Personal identity, defined by race, religion, ethnicity, and gender, presents particular difficulties for those wanting to lead effectively. Who is in the room and how their diverse identities affect the quality of proceedings and product command considerably more attention in the present work context than they did in the past. Differing perceptions about these matters can distort proceedings and detract from product quality unless group members open themselves to defining the forms of diversity that are most important to them and identify handles of respect that each member of a group can grasp. Failing this, what might have been powerful assets within a group faced with an assigned task may turn readily into disabling deficits that paralyze a group and make failure a foregone conclusion.

Although the case has already been made that a variety of people concerned with the quality of organizational functioning in multiple sectors might benefit from reading this book, exactly who is it aimed at? At the top of the list are people seeking to become more adept at enhancing the learning of those who aspire to leadership in organizations. Included are leading executives in corporations, government agencies, and not-for-profit organizations. Increasingly, they see it as one of their highest priorities to develop the leadership capacities of the people working with them. A growing number of organizations also see themselves as being actively involved in the teaching of leadership.

Individuals and groups responsible for designing and implementing leadership development efforts will benefit from the teachings in this book. In this category are those who have responsibility in their organizations for human resource development, as well as those who come in from the outside to assist with professional or staff development, either from a university or from a consulting firm.

At the same time, just about anybody interested in the improved functioning of organizations, large or small, will find the material presented here useful and compelling. It will give them not only a lot to think about in terms of professional and organizational development but a number of things they can actually try out, if they are willing to brave some new terrain. They will become more aware of the tremendous energy that lies beneath the surface of the daily grind, energy that springs as much from the spirits as from the minds of people who work in organizations.

If their experience approximates mine in any way, they will also become swept up in the positive potential that inheres in nearly every organizational context. Being able to overcome differences and work together for common cause is a repetitive theme of all the shared experiences presented here.

Following this introduction is a chapter that places experiential leadership development in context. Integral is my own thinking about teaching leadership, as well as the thinking of others who have addressed the topic before me. In essence, I situate my own philosophy and approach in the appropriate literature, both historical and contemporary. The origins of ideas are important. Like the missions of organizations at the time they were chartered, origins illuminate purpose. Clarity of purpose is a large part of what I am trying to achieve in this book.

The book then turns decidedly more practical with the introduction of the 25 exercises. This is accomplished in a chapter that puts forth a series of cues that people can follow as they think about doing experiential leadership development. In the succeeding four chapters, each headed by one of the major organizational challenges—risking innovation, fostering collaboration, managing conflict, and using diversity—I present the 25 exercises. For each one there is an initial piece on purpose, a set of explicit instructions on how to prepare for and carry out the activity, comments that guide users toward successful application or at least provide indications of successful application, a brief treatment of strategic considerations regarding the use of the exercise, and a full outline of discussion questions for facilitators to achieve an effective debrief.

The chapter following those on the exercises presents a real-life story that demonstrates the use of the exercises within an organizational development initiative. The story is about building capacity in a government agency so that it can better serve its mission in a rapidly changing environment both outside and inside the organization. It is a composite story, crafted from experiences I have had assisting various clients. Discussion and commentary follow a description of the initiative and point out major considerations regarding fit applications. Finally, a short chapter recaps the progression of ideas in the book.

First Encounters with Versions of the
Activities Nested in the Exercises

- Spacejam, Magic Steps, Working Norms, Innovation Maze, and Mapping Diversity: I learned versions of these activities from a graduate assistant, Craig Imler, who worked with me on the first graduate leadership class I taught at Michigan State University. I believe that the root of Working Norms is something called A Full Value Contract devised by Project Adventure, which originated in Massachusetts.

- Fishbowl Consultant, Towering Vision, Voices: I was introduced to a version of these activities during a project on which I served as a consultant. Its aim was to develop collaborative skills among a group seeking to advance the cause of sustainable agriculture in Michigan in the early 1990s. My first introduction to the activity in Towering Vision was through an instruction sheet that originated with Blue Ridge Resource Group of North Carolina in 1993.

- Concentric Conversations: Although colleagues tell me they have seen this activity done by others, I devised a version of it myself for work with extension agents at Michigan State University.

- Discussion Functions, Tug of War, and Listening in More Than One Voice: These activities grew out of discussions between me and a teaching colleague at Michigan State University, Diane Holt-Reynolds. She was a more generative force than I on all three.

- Planning From the Ground Up, Marking Effective Teamwork: Although colleagues tell me they have seen the first of these activities done by others, I devised a version of both myself for work with graduate students at Michigan State University and with a corporate client.

- My Spot: I learned the activity from an Outward Bound instructor who was engaged as a consultant on a special project I was involved with at Michigan State University, Dave McGough.

- Shaping the Future: I cannot honestly remember my first encounter with this activity, although I dimly recollect a connection with Dave McGough. It is also known by the title Blind Polygram, or just Blind Poly.

- Witch and Watch, Diversity Bingo, and Stereotypes: I became acquainted with these activities in leadership academies sponsored by a Michigan education reform group with which I worked. Various presenters used versions of them on the programs we presented.

- Bureaucracy: I first experienced this activity in a parking lot in the middle of a top management retreat I was leading as head of Hurricane Island Outward Bound. There is a brief write-up of it in Rohnke (1984), p. 122.

- Evacuation Drill: I first experienced a version of this activity while a participant on an Outward Bound course at Hurricane Island.

- Leaders' Walk and the Being: I cannot remember my first encounter with these activities. I learned the former as Sherpa Walk.

- Ritual Conflict: I have already credited Michael Brown for the key aspects of the activity.

CHAPTER 1

Ways of Thinking About Leadership Development

This chapter explores the terrain of contemporary initiatives in leadership development, critiques the assumptions on which they are based, and makes a case for the more cost-effective deployment of experiential approaches to educating leaders.

The Nature of the Subject

Leadership development is about teaching leadership. The role of teacher is to create and carry out a mix of activities that will have a positive effect on learners in terms of the subject being taught. In the contemporary context, the subject of leadership requires learners to become adept at shaping and fulfilling not only their own aims but those of their followers as well. As James O'Toole (1995) notes in *Leading Change,* leadership based on imposing one's will on others increasingly engenders negative rather than positive effects.

Instrumental to leadership development is a wide range of aptitudes and capabilities, all of which affect a person's interactions with coworkers, constituents, or customers—personal qualities, moral commitments, and management skills. The effects of leadership development are most directly felt in the social setting of an organization, where leaders and followers attempt to work together to attain common goals (Terry, 1993).

Over the past century, as organizations have grown and their numbers have spread across the landscape of human endeavor, concern with leadership development has widened and deepened. In fact, it is fair to say that the quality of leadership available to organizations and institutions has reached the threshold of becoming a major preoccupation within industrialized nations. This should not be surprising, because the performance of the people in charge is rather consequential, when most of us depend on the entities they lead for both our sustenance and our sense of well-being. To merit the label *preoccupation,* an issue must draw considerable comment over a sustained period from experts and others with enough time on their hands to find a public outlet for their opinions. Like the proverbial elephant, the issue must supply enough mass for pundits to be able to step back, take sightings, and assert, with little fear of contradiction, that they have described a substantial part of what is in front of them. The topic of leadership development admirably fulfills these requirements. A cursory reading of the trade journals reveals extensive discussion of various parts of the ample bulk of the leadership development elephant.

Current Dimensions

There are four major dimensions to leadership development. Taken together, they represent a useful way of fitting the parts of the elephant into a manageable frame.

- *Who* should do leadership development

- *When,* or within what time frame, it should be done

- *Where* should leadership development occur, or on whose turf experiences should be organized

- *How* should it unfold, or *what* materials and methods should be used to teach leadership

Who?

Four decades ago, the answer unequivocally would have been that university professors should teach leadership, especially those in business and public administration, and perhaps also in education. In the past 30 years, however, consultants have become an established and significant part of the leadership teaching corps. Their principal leverage in the field derives from an ability to respond much more quickly and directly than the professoriat to expressed needs within the workplace itself. To such immediacy the academy never intended nor was equipped to respond: Universities continue to concentrate on the long-term development of leaders, separate from the specific organizational context in which they work. Consultants can focus more on the short-term development of groups faced with specific challenges within an organizational setting.

Recently, increasing sentiment has been voiced that neither professors nor consultants can do the job of teaching leadership as well as executives or leaders themselves. Accepting the criticism of present-day leadership development as "too rote, too backward-looking, too theoretical" (Cohen & Tichy, 1997, p. 73), several leading thinkers make the case that organizational leaders themselves should take responsibility for developing leaders at all levels in their organizations. In one groundbreaking approach, executives themselves formulate their own stories about "ideas, values, edge, and energy," and they share them with subordinates in the firm. Drawn from their own experience, the stories become the principal tools for building coworkers' leadership skills and capacities (Cohen & Tichy, 1997).

The matter of who should do leadership development has some obvious appeal in that it identifies, albeit innocuously, heroes and villains and designates ownership rights. There is really not much of substance to the issue itself, however. In many, if not most, instances, individuals of similar background wind up with central roles as teachers; it just so happens that they are at different points in their careers when they are engaged as such.

A common scenario is the former executive who becomes a consultant and then a part-time professor, before turning into an executive again, only to close out a career as a professor or consultant. The edge that a professor might bring to leadership development, as opposed to a consultant or an executive, is solely one of perspective and breadth of understanding. These are related as much to the requisites of what should be done and how as to who does it.

In the example cited above, Cohen and Tichy (1997) assert a prominent role for executives in leadership development, but it is their own frame, not the executives', that supplies direction for the program. When analysts offer a prominent position to the question of who should do leadership development, they are really using it as a way of provoking questions about content and methodology.

When?

Should the teaching of leadership be in short bursts of time or drawn out over longer periods? How much sustained, continuous time should be allocated? Should the time allocated to formal instruction be interspersed among longer periods of on-the-job experience, whether through organized practice sessions or through apprenticeships?

Just as the matter of who cannot be separated from the question of what and how, neither can the matter of when. Time and timing are critical adjuncts of content and methodology because they connect to the question of sequencing and its close partner, cumulative effects. That a project group can handle with great facility a charged issue involving ethnic differences is more than a matter of good fortune. Such facility has roots in the group's prior learning. Perhaps it was fostered through a series of seemingly inconsequential setup exercises experienced in the first week the group spent together. The effect of proper sequencing will become apparent from the exercise descriptions provided later in Chapters 2 through 6.

With more time, there can be greater influence if the learning challenges are the right ones and they are ordered properly. Interspersing periods of instruction with periods of practice, stage-setting activity, or just plain fun may be the best use of available time. Letting discomfiting new ideas settle and take hold in a real work context and then later in a more remote environment, asking participants to reexamine and reshape their thinking in light of recent on-the-job experience may be the most effective ordering of elements.

A solid and enduring commitment to collaboration, for example, cannot be molded solely in the hothouse setting of a training center, or even in the more natural milieu of the workplace itself. Carefully interweaving experiences in both settings over time might produce the desired effects. The determinant of when to do something is what to do and how to carry it off.

Where?

Should leadership development activities take place in a university classroom? Or in a retreat center off the work site? Or perhaps in special training facilities at the work site? Or in unfamiliar wilderness settings, or even more remote venues such as soup kitchens? Or in the work settings of other organizations doing the same kind of work as those undergoing training? Clearly the options are more diverse today than they have ever been. Leaderless groups in a pleasant rural setting, team building aboard rubber rafts on a fast-running river, and service projects in the underground haunts of the homeless in a large city now complement expert lectures and Socratic give-and-take offered in amphitheater-style classrooms of noted business schools. Undersea or outer space may be the only frontiers left untapped.

The question of place, like that of who offers leadership education and in what time frame, is subsidiary to decision making about content and methodology. A program designer does not a priori decide that it would be beneficial to take a group of middle managers into the outback for 2 weeks of sustained team leadership training. There is usually an aim in mind, whether well- or ill-conceived, explicit or implicit, and choice of place relates to how best to achieve that aim. The outback can offer participants all the educational advantages of considerable discomfort, just as a lush resort can offer all the educational advantages of comfort. Either one or both could be essential for learning, or conversely, could stand in the way of learning. It all depends on the objectives; and objectives govern content and methodology.

Increasingly, those who teach leadership seek to fit place to purpose, and in many instances to alternate places depending on different purposes. Integrated, 3-week programs can take place in several different venues. They might begin with a short stint in the wilderness, followed by classroom or retreat center sessions, and then involve a move to an urban site for service projects. The current literature on leadership development is replete with descriptions of programs that take place in multiple sites. For example, Albert Vicere (1996) describes three very differently configured programs—the Center for Creative Leadership's Leaderlab, AT&T's Leadership Development Program, and Aramark's Executive Leadership Institute. Each offers locales that purportedly complement the aims they are seeking to achieve.

What and How?

The central concerns for those designing and doing leadership development are objectives, content, and methodology. These are the wellsprings of a program. They determine the quality of the experiences participants have. Ultimately the effect on participants, in terms of what they do in the workplace, stems from these. If the what and how are solid, they can actually overcome deficiencies in the where and when, and perhaps even the who. But the reverse is not the case.

From the point of view of the participants, the principal vehicles for leadership development, in terms of content and methodology, include the following:

- Listening to a lecture

- Engaging in discussion with peers, alone or with coaches or consultants

- Pursuing a formal dialogue (Bohm, 1990) with peers, supervisors, supervisees, or some combination of these

- Analyzing a case study of another organization's problems or one's own

- Going through a short or long experience with peers, supervisors, supervisees, or some combination of these, and then debriefing it. The shared experience could be drawn from one's own workplace or someone else's. Or it could be constructed from natural circumstances like the ones a wilderness setting provides, or artificial ones like those conjured in games and simulations.

- Discussing with a coach or mentor designated problems

- Undergoing a leadership assessment, either via a survey instrument or through expert observation of behavior, exhibited either on the job or in a lab setting

Naturally, any one of these experiences can take on one or more characteristics, depending on desired content specifications. The material that participants engage with, for example, could be highly theoretical or quite practical. At the same time, it could span both, by prodding participants to formulate mental models of the behavior they exhibit on the job (Argyris, 1992; Senge, 1990) or providing them with open-ended opportunities to assess their effectiveness as professionals (Schon, 1983). Alternatively, the material might encourage participants to generate and try out new ideas and concepts, or it could focus specifically on past actions and the determination of immediate next steps in the workplace.

In another vein altogether, some of what is put in front of participants might relate to their particular work environment. Although still reflective of real-world challenges, the material could include issues and problems that obtain in a wide range of settings. On the other hand, it might on its face have little apparent relevance to particular organizational contexts, or even to issues or problems that broadly diverse participants see as germane to their work situations. In contrast, the content could be timeless and enduring, relating to how human beings face a variety of challenges that transcend any organizational milieu. Taking a different perspective altogether, it might be tied to this year's work plan and have little foreseeable effect beyond that time frame.

Closing out the range of possibilities, the material could be quite technical or scientific, involving the acquisition of so-called hard skills. If not purely technical, its principal attribute could be its objectivity, with the consequent presence or absence of attainable skills easily discernable by observation or survey. In contrast, the material in front of participants could emphasize the personal and interpersonal, involving so-called soft skills, touching on the emotional and perhaps even the spiritual dimensions of getting a job done.

From the Literature, Some Misleading Assumptions

It ought to be abundantly apparent from the options just offered that the content and methodology of leadership development make up a deep and thick wood. This should serve as ample warning that thoughtfulness to the point of rigor and care to the point of compassion should obtain. Regrettably, content and methodology have not received the judicious treatment they deserve. The contemporary literature on leadership development—as represented in recent issues of *Organizational Dynamics* (Burke, 1997; Conger, 1993; Raelin, 1997), *Across the Board* (Csoka, 1996), the *Journal of Management Development* (Keys, 1990; Wells, 1990), and the *Journal of Management* (Keys, 1988)—betrays a coverage of these critical dimensions that is superficial at best.

This superficiality is most apparent in the assumptions made about the most appropriate means of developing leadership capacity. Conveyed as if they were givens offering essential guidance for program development, these assumptions include the following:

- Issues and problems drawn from the workplace of the participants provide the most fruitful learning challenges for contemporary leadership development.

- Experiential learning activities, organized in one form or another outside traditional instructional settings, are generally better than learning activities that are classroom-based activities.

- A highly diverse program that includes a market basket of methodologies is generally superior to an approach that is one dimensional.

- The who, when, and where of program development deserve the same level of attention as the what and how.

The problem with these assumptions is not that they are flatly false. Quite the contrary, there is a good deal of validity in them. Their principal defect is that they are misleading: They do not point the way to the most artful and cost-effective leadership development treatments. The first assumption is that the most fitting material for leadership development is the problems and issues that dominate in the workplace of the participants. Rather than invalidating the assumption outright, it is fitting to offer the simple rejoinder, drawn from tenets of good teaching, that participants in leadership development programs should spend as much time away from workplace problems and issues as they do in their midst. They could benefit equally from grappling with unfamiliar circumstances as from dealing with familiar ones. Assuredly, the unfamiliar should contain elements reminiscent enough to touch responsive chords in the participants. At the same time, differences should aid participants in overcoming dysfunctional patterns that plague them in the workplace.

It might seem that the second assumption, the desirability of experiential learning away from a classroom-type setting, is counter to many of the downsides stemming from the first. Unfortunately, as the literature itself demonstrates, this is not the case. Experiential in most instances in the literature means "exotic," a set of experiences conducted off-site, from which participants are supposed to glean important lessons they can then bring back to their workplace. In essence, what is offered as experiential is the experience in and of itself, usually an activity involving high intensity and high cost. A week at an Outward Bound program for 20 top managers is a fitting example.

The nub of the problem with program decisions predicated on the second assumption is they are an "expensive half-loaf," not very much better than "no loaf at all." Although participant experience is certainly central to leadership development, it must contain not only a set of activities but also an effective means of distilling the learning that the activities promote. The only way this can happen is if an able teacher assists participants with concept formation and possible application to their workplace. Well-facilitated discussion is central to an experience, not supplementary. It captures the learning and makes appropriate connections with the workplace.

As important, experiential does not have to mean extreme, remote, and costly. It can mean mild, proximate, and inexpensive. Low-intensity experiences provided within the four walls of a classroom can lead to vigorous discussions, with great potential for leadership learning. It is often unnecessary to take a group away for an intensive, week-long training session in the wilderness. With a group that is ready, several hours of active engagement with a well-chosen exercise in an ample-sized room can produce marked effects. The exercises described later provide strong testimony on this point.

On the third assumption, there is no doubt that highly diversified leadership development treatments can make for rich learning opportunities. A week of Outward Bound, followed by a week of lectures and discussions on a university campus, and a final week of a service project in an urban center may be the right mix to create effect. The other side of the coin is that such programs may be overdone, full of costly moves that are not necessary for the achievement of a specific set of objectives. Much preferred are exquisitely differentiated objectives, clearly articulated at the outset, with targeted responses by way of proposed activities. To do things this way, hard-nosed design work is essential, with its primary focus the content and methodology of a program, tied cleanly to a set of explicit purposes.

I have already explained in full above why the fourth assumption misleads—that is, putting the who, where, and when on a par with the what and how. It is important, however, to add here that directing the eye away from content and methodology increases the possibility that they will remain underexamined. If the attention is dispersed, then the amount of inquiry directed at any one element will likely be insufficient. This is the case with the present state of the literature on leadership development.

Unfortunate Consequences of Being Misled

Unfortunate consequences accompany actions based on the four assumptions. Topping the list, program quality has suffered, and the costs of putting on leadership development programs have become needlessly exorbitant. Loss of quality is the result of not tying activity tightly to purpose. Fine-grained decision making about the least expensive yet most effective means to an end is not occurring. Excess is the result of making leadership development programs into conglomerations of what's and how's, the total cost of which is frequently unjustifiable.

In stark contrast, strong cumulative effect on participants can be achieved if the following are present: careful attention is paid to the choice and sequencing of program elements; an understanding is exhibited of participants' needs for trying out new ideas on safe ground, away from their workplace; a right balance is struck between wrestling with ideas on an individual basis as opposed to a group basis; and patience is shown in terms of bringing the issues back home to the workplace. Failure to make the right moves and to effect the right order of moves inevitably leads to redundancies and to the needless expenditure of resources.

The demand for better leaders and consequently for more expansive leadership development efforts is strong and likely to become stronger in the years ahead. In this accelerating rush to create new and better programs, many sponsors and designers have let their appetites for grandiosity overtake their penchant for good judgment. Lost is deference to the principle that well-crafted, modest interventions targeted to achievable ends and tied to broader, long-range aims may in the end produce more profoundly positive and enduring effects.

What is needed is a grounded presentation that ties activities to objectives; that is explicit about objectives, content, and methodology; that offers solid substance for leaders, trainers, and others who teach leadership. The overarching goal should be to preserve and extend the advancements contained in the present set of initiatives, while setting aside the costly fluff. Inevitably, the blush will come off the rose of leadership development in its current forms, and organizational leaders will seek out more refined and economical approaches, decrying the excesses of the current array.

A Wiser Path

In comparison to efforts that share the same purpose, the treatments offered in this book are effective yet inexpensive. A variety of people in diverse sectors can be educated or can educate themselves to do the suggested exercises. With good design assistance, they can also address critical questions of sequencing and fit with other leadership development efforts, on-site and off-site. Allotted time necessary is for the most part fairly minimal—a half hour to a half day for each exercise. Adequate setting and props can be managed comfortably within the tightest budget. If the exercises are used at the right time in the right place with amenable participants, the results can be remarkably cost-effective.

The ideas that undergird treatments like the ones exemplified in this book are not new. They have been with us for decades but have remained to a large extent unexplored and unexploited. Lately an increasing number of leading thinkers (Bolman & Deal, 1994; Clarke & Clarke, 1994) have pressed for greater attention to experiential forms of leadership development. Before turning to a description of the exercises, it is important to explain the origins of this thinking as it has emerged in my mind and in the literature.

The primary "text" participants in leadership development programs should study, in my view, is shared experience. Needless to say, this sort of text is very different from that which is purchased in a bookstore, a package of ideas contained between two covers. Experience is raw and immediate, messy and open-ended. As such, it places unusual demands on all who seek to use it for learning and further professional development. Yet, when appropriately facilitated, its potential as a learning tool is limitless.

The role of teacher-leader is to have participants reflect more carefully on what they do together and make connections with what they do outside in the real world. Primarily from their reflections on experience—provoked with carefully phrased and sequenced questions—participants can begin to reconstruct, reform, and revise their ideas about the practice of organizational leadership. Only secondarily and as a support should reference be made to the body of expert opinion found in books and articles as we inquire together into the meaning of our experiences. In fact, it is worth remembering that expert commentary is often nothing more than the result of experts' carefully reflecting on their own experiences.

Make no mistake, the "bridging leap" asked of participants here is enormous. From dwelling with a teacher and with each other on their experiences to forming and attaching themselves to new concepts of leadership and management that they can bring into their workplace—this involves considerable reach and strain. Yet one can be assured that if participants become emotionally engaged—discomfited or satisfied, pleased or concerned, agitated or composed—because of what is happening around and to them; if their attitudes and those of their peers can remain unfrozen, even if momentarily; and if they begin to make initial connections between their own experience in an exercise and new ideas about what might make sense to do at work, the positive effect on them will be significant and enduring.

The ready order that emerges from an instructor expounding a specific idea or set of ideas is not present in the approach just described. Therefore, focus is more difficult to attain. But if it is attained, albeit haltingly, through emotion-filled and value-laden direct experience, the hold of the new ideas on participants will be much more secure (Proudman, 1992). The bricks—that is, good ideas—will not only be in place, they will be secured with ample mortar—that is, accompanying feelings and attitudes.

Contrast the approach just described, for example, with "receiving the word" from noted experts, in person, on a big screen, or via the written word. Although expert opinion, however conveyed, is targeted and lucid, it is less likely to promote altered practices. However cogent it might be, it is inevitably sterile in that it is detached from the lives of the participants.

The Roots of Experiential Learning

In laboring in these fields, one should be acutely aware of borrowing the ideas of others. Foremost is John Dewey, whose *Education and Experience* (1938) is seminal. Offered first as a lecture to a professional society, it set the stage for most of the expert commentary on experiential learning that followed. To Dewey, "every experience enacted and undergone, modifies the one who acts and undergoes, while this modification affects, whether we wish it or not, the quality of subsequent experiences" (p. 35).

Dewey (1938) offers two interrelated principles, or criteria, of experience that lend themselves well to anyone who wants to capitalize on experience for learning. The first is continuity, the second is interaction. The idea of continuity is that experiences build on each other. "Every experience is a moving force. Its value can be judged only on the ground of what it moves toward and into" (Dewey, 1938, p. 38). The idea of interaction is that experience involves a person with what is around him or her. "An experience is always what it is because of a transaction taking place between an individual and his environment" (p. 43), whether other people, an issue, a book, or whatever constitutes that environment. Within the frame of these transactions the rich drama of human impulses, needs and desires unfolds, and from it people seek a sense of purpose and meaning. Notes Dewey, humans are by nature not satisfied with merely observing experience. Their impulses, needs, and desires compel them to understand its significance, and ultimately push them toward a sense of purpose. "A purpose is an end-view" (p. 68).

> The formation of purposes . . . involves (1) observation of surrounding conditions; (2) knowledge of what has happened in similar situations in the past . . . and (3) judgment which puts

together what is observed and what is recalled to see what they signify. (p. 69)

The principles of continuity and interaction in experience and the inevitable march to a sense of purpose are central to the dynamics thoughtful leadership teachers should seek to create in the space chosen for leadership learning, be it a meeting room of a hotel, the spacious lawn of a nearby park, or an academic classroom. These spaces are ample for common experiences in the form of group exercises, simulations, or problems. Specially designed and constructed, they are meant to pose significant leadership quandaries. Contrary to what many might say, they are not "fake" or "unreal" experiences. As "a rose is a rose," an experience is an experience, whether it occurs in an office, on the way home from work, or in a classroom or training center.

The difference between constructed experience and that of everyday work life is that the former takes place in a fashioned lab setting away from the multiple demands of the latter. It is consciously removed from the demands and norms of the work environment. Such experiences allow people time and space to reflect on their own behavior, in somewhat less precarious circumstances than those where jobs and reputations are at stake. In effect, they take place on safe ground, often essential for people to open themselves to learning.

In his landmark work, *The Reflective Practitioner,* Don Schon (1983) offers strong substantiation of the need for safe ground, especially when important leadership capacities such as risk taking and collaboration are at stake. Schon argues for the expanded exercise of what he calls reflection-in-action by professionals. This capacity goes beyond technical expertise, inviting a professional to respond to uncertain and complex circumstances by surfacing key operating assumptions and analyzing them even in the middle of ongoing work.

From one of the cases he presents, Schon (1983) concludes that "the reflection-in-action of managers is distinctive in that they operate in an organizational context and deal with organizational phenomena," which involve "a system of games and norms which both guide and limit the directions of organizational inquiry" (p. 265). In situations where managers must take certain actions to preserve their position and image, these games and norms become "diseases that prevent their own cure" (p. 266). The effects on organizational performance are inevitably negative.

Schon's (1983) account beckons the creation of circumstances in which people who aspire to leadership are compelled to take a larger view, to look more at the big picture and at underlying assumptions driving actions and reactions, in a setting removed from the disabling games and norms of the organizations in which they work. Such conditions provide participants with a necessary opportunity to work through the multiple, intertwined observations of experiential phenomena.

The intent is to advance the level and quality of those observations to the point where participants begin to engage in serious reflection-in-action, and ultimately in the formation of new concepts. The work that facilitator and participants do together in this context becomes an exercise in "hyperobservation," leading to an analysis of working assumptions (theories-in-action) and to a reframing of operating principles, ground rules that govern future action. It is axiomatic that such a progression cannot take place within the confines of an organization's work space. The fresh air of experiential exercises conducted off the work site offers an efficient way of surfacing working assumptions for serious review and revision.

Endemic to effective interaction with participants in the exercises is drawing them up short, into an analysis of "what has just taken place in this room." The situation that has just arisen is held up as a manifestation of an issue or problem that has to be dealt with outside this room, in the real world. To repeat an earlier contention, the experience participants and teacher are having in the exercise and discussion following is not artificial; it is as real as that which occurs elsewhere.

This is particularly true of a topic such as leadership, at the very heart of which is social interaction, definition of purpose, accomplishment of task, and evaluation of results. Such ingredients are as much in evidence in the room participants are meeting in as in their workplaces. There may, in actuality, be more potential for solid learning from the here and now, in contrast to the "home base," remote as the latter is in the heat of the moment.

Conclusion

This chapter focuses on essential aspects of leadership development, which at core is about teaching leadership. It recounts four dimensions of leadership development and fixes on the central one, content and methodology. It then uncovers several major operating assumptions that prevail in the current literature. Rather than serving as a useful guide to effective practice, these assumptions can mislead practitioners in significant ways. The costs of being misled are high, in terms of both effectiveness and monetary outlay.

Having laid bare central deficiencies apparent in the present thinking about leadership development, I put forth a different way of conceptualizing. This approach capitalizes on the promise that exists in present initiatives, such as group experiential learning; yet at the same time, it avoids pitfalls, such as overly elaborate experiences whose effects are weak for the expense incurred. In the end, the chapter points the way to more leadership learning for less expense, rather than the reverse.

CHAPTER 2

Cueing the Exercises

In this chapter, I offer ideas and suggestions about how to prepare for and carry out the 25 exercises that are described in full detail in the succeeding chapters. If followed, these procedural cues can assist mightily with appropriate use and successful application. The cues reinforce many of the ideas already presented on experiential forms of leadership development. It is important to remember, however, that there is no precise formula for achieving desired results. As with all forms of teaching, trial and error, followed by retrial, is the only path that leads anywhere worth going.

Although not a hard-and-fast rule, facilitators should allocate considerably more time to preparation for an exercise than to the exercise itself—perhaps as much as double the amount of time. The three elements that are most critical to the success of an exercise are the setup, that is, selecting an appropriate space and positioning participants; the directions given participants; and the debrief, the group discussion that follows the activity part of the exercise.

The setup is the entryway for participants to the unfamiliar space of the exercise. The directions are the explanatory greeting they receive as they stand at the threshold of that space. The two together provide an initial look at the space and a set of cues about what participants will be allowed to do and not do while in it. Some of the cues will be explicit, some subtle, some the result of a lack of reference altogether. The one mentioned last is in effect cueing through omission.

The debrief is the bridge between the activity and participants' learning—between their experiencing the activity and their mental formulations with regard to organizational functioning in general, and the functioning of their own organization in particular. The facilitator stands as a guide on this bridge, to assist participants in making connections between what they just experienced in an activity and what for many may be unfamiliar ways of thinking about organizational functioning. The facilitator also guides participants to make connections between the experience and the more familiar space of their own organization.

In effect, the debrief is a relatively compact period in which participants pause and reflect, where initial observations, perspectives, and attitudes are unpacked and laid out for all to examine, and where in the final analysis meaning and value are assigned.

Preparing for the Exercises

Here are agenda items for the extensive preparation that is recommended:

- Which exercise should be used and why? This is a top consideration that deserves much forethought. Why should you, for example, do Bureaucracy now? What are you trying to achieve? Which objectives are you seeking to accomplish? Do these objectives make sense in the present context and at the present moment for the group in question? Are structural encumbrances that hamper working group progress, Bureaucracy's focus, a problem that should be addressed now?
- Can you fulfill your objectives with this group of participants? Who are they? Where are they are in their development, as individuals and as a working group? Will they likely benefit from experiencing this exercise now?
- Which activities will engage them, as opposed to boring them or repelling them—accepting that there are times when the latter two reactions may be instrumental in promoting learning? Discomfort or unease can be useful as long as it does not engender mutiny. The applicable decision rule is whether the activity is likely to produce a vigorous and intense debrief. The quality of the debrief is a much better indicator of the appropriateness of an exercise than the participants' enjoyment of the activity in and of itself.
- Where does a given exercise fit within a professional development sequence? Such sequences normally include a number of elements, from wrestling with challenges experienced on the job, to an array of off-site learning activities, to experiential exercises conducted on- or off-site? Magic Steps coming on the heels of a group's determination of vision and strategy may be just the right boost to propel it toward imaginative and productive moves in the workplace.

Innovation Maze in advance of a critical project requiring total group commitment may effect exactly the sort of cohesion needed.

• What pace is appropriate, and how should you deal with likely time constraints? Can you really do the Tower in 45 minutes—what would the outcomes look like if you had to compress the exercise into such a brief period? Would you have to compress the debrief so much that the opportunity for initial learning would essentially be lost?

• What connections are you hoping participants will make when you select a particular exercise? Is the exercise more useful for participants to form new concepts about organizational issues in general, or is it more useful for their identification of particular approaches to the challenges they face in the workplace? Might the exercise serve both purposes equally well, given a generous allotment of time for the debrief? Ritual Conflict, for example, is an excellent platform for concept formation about an area that is unfamiliar to many who work in organizations, effective conflict management. Yet, exploring potential workplace applications requires quite sophisticated participants and substantial debriefing time. The key determinants are context and constraints, where a group is in its development, and what will be most useful to that group at a given point.

• Should you supplement an exercise with a leadership inventory, a formal assessment of individual or group capabilities, or both? It usually intensifies the learning for participants if they are asked to reflect not only on what they did in an activity but also on what they gleaned from an assessment about their own inclinations or attributes. The effects of Towering Vision, for example, are intensified if you join it with an inventory of participants' collaborative leadership capacities (Kaagan & Donahue, 1996) or some other tools that taps into the capacities the exercise highlights.

Doing the Exercises

Suggestions on doing the exercises follow.

• You will need to collect all necessary gear and props beforehand, making sure that appropriate adaptations are made well in advance. If you leave the uniquely fashioned bingo cards for Diversity Bingo behind in your office, the result will be no exercise. If you fail to adapt the questions on the cards to the needs and interests of the participants, there might as well be no exercise.

• Make sure the amount of physical space is sufficient and all the furnishings are arrayed appropriately. Attempting Concentric Conversations with 15 groups of 12 each in a room full of lunch tables piled high with dirty dishes is dysfunctional—not to mention messy.

• You should practice direction giving for the exercise until you get it right. This point is important and warrants considerable discussion. When you as facilitator are telling participants the rules at the outset of an exercise, you are enumerating for them the factors that govern behavior in "another world," the world of the exercise. Just as the real world has rules such as not stealing a neighbor's goods, Discussion Functions has rules such as keeping quiet after having exhausted one's supply of cards. Rules, or the absence of them, in an exercise parallel real-world constraints; although they are artificial to some extent, they are meant to simulate conditions that inhibit freedom of action.

It is critical that as facilitator you not only explain the constraints clearly but also omit verbal references to behavior that should be left to participants' discretion. The latter is where participants have latitude to do as they wish. Not saying that something is against the rules means that it is allowed. In spite of this, that is, something being allowed, participants often assume that particular actions are prohibited within an activity. This is to be expected. We all tend to assume constraints where there are none, not only in the context of exercises but in real organizational contexts as well. In Star Wars, participants' assumption that they should remain on their feet bars them from responding creatively to imposed constraints, despite the fact that the directions make no mention of whether participants have to stay on their feet.

Assumptions made about constraints are excellent fodder for discussion in the debrief. Also intriguing and worth discussion is that participants frequently break the explicit rules of an activity as opposed to using the considerable discretion offered in what is not prohibited in the initial rule giving.

This whole area, the assumptions that participants make about what is allowed or not allowed, is a mine of opportunities for a facilitator. Unlocking these opportunities, however, depends on the quality of the direction setting. If as facilitator you present the rules and "nothing but" the rules, you will lay the ground for a powerful debrief. The issue of the latitude that participants have for innovation and risk taking can receive the full airing that it deserves. This can set the stage for participants' making sharper distinctions about actual as opposed to imagined constraints faced on the job, as well as how they might more imaginatively confront those that are real.

• If you have not done an exercise before—and it is critical you do it well—find a few friends on whom to practice direction giving before you have to do it live. You will be surprised at the details your friends will tell you you overlooked in the practice run. Even if you have done an exercise before, discussing the in's and out's of an exercise with other people is always helpful. Because the exercises are live and totally interactive, prior interaction with a sympathetic human being can be very useful before going into a situation full of demanding and expectant, and perhaps paying, participants.

• In the conduct of the exercise, it is important to understand that participants are likely to behave in unpredictable ways as the activity unfolds. They will in effect do with it as they wish, not necessarily as you wish. Your job for the most part is to get out of the way and let them do it, knowing always that the debrief provides ample opportunity to discuss what happened.

The appropriate approach may include allowing participants to "break the rules," that is, go beyond the constraints inherent in the exercise. Although there are times that you might want to rein them in from going so far outside the rules as to invalidate the effects of the exercise—escaping its challenges—a laissez-faire attitude is generally the most advisable.

For beginning facilitators, a laissez-faire approach may be difficult. The tendency is to want to save the participants from failing or from doing it all wrong. In general, facilitators should vigorously resist the temptation to intervene. Only moves or gestures that keep participants "in the game," however much they seem to straying from the "right answer," should be undertaken by the facilitator.

For example, in observing groups struggle with the Innovation Maze, I am tempted to use body language to get supporters to array themselves around the maze when an innovator is attempting to pick his or her way through it. I have to restrain myself consciously, reminding myself not to deprive participants of any part of their experience. My job is help them understand later, in the debrief, what they did and what it means.

• What if some of the participants have done the activity before? Take consolation in the strong likelihood that they will not have done it in the same manner as they will do it with you. It matters little whether someone has done an activity previously. At a deeper level, the exercise as a whole is not about building a newspaper tower, or threading people through a masking tape maze on the floor, or leading a group of blindfolded people through the halls of a hotel complex. It is about essential capacities that groups and organizations must develop if they are to be productive and successful. The understanding that you can promote in an effective debrief, different from any such discussion participants have had before, is limitless.

If, perchance, there is a solution in the activity that you fear experienced participants will reveal to others, tell them not to, that it will deprive others of valuable learning they have already had. In addition, urge the person to push themselves to get better at overcoming the challenges the exercise presents. Suggest too that they hone their observation skills about what others are doing because they need not concentrate as much on the problem the activity presents. Tell them that you will be depending on them for expert observations in the debrief, and then ask for these observations as the debrief unfolds.

The Debrief

There are generally three sequential steps a facilitator takes participants through to analyze an activity and extrapolate ideas from it. Although the debrief is demarcated from the activity itself, the separation of one from another is rather artificial. The debrief is just as much a part of the fabric of the experience for the participants as the activity itself. It is, as Dewey might have construed it, the experience that elaborates or attenuates the experience. From the point of view of the participants—not unimportant here—both the activity and the back and forth that develops immediately afterward run as one fluid in their veins and brain cells, influencing both physical and mental states as if they were one.

The three steps are what happened, implications, and applications.

- What happened involves a recitation of what actually occurred within the confines of the activity; who did what to whom and in what order.

- Implications derive from an examination of the meaning of what just happened, the interpretations that can legitimately be drawn from the experience, particularly in terms of the functioning of organizations and the practice of leadership.

- Applications relate to what participants should do differently from here on in because of what was just learned, that is, how what was learned from the experience ought to be translated into what happens upon return to the workplace.

Much of the three, what happened, implications, and applications, reach across the extensive and rich terrain that only direct experience can provide: feelings, attitudes, and ideas. Questions such as the following corroborate this:

- What was it like to do such and such?

- What was your reaction to so and so taking charge?

- What was your attitude toward the group's reaching rapid consensus?

- What was the nub of the task presented in the exercise?

- What did you perceive to be the purpose of the activity?

- What was your sense of who exerted good judgment at particularly critical junctures?

Finally, the three steps offer a natural continuum of experience itself. What happened looks to the immediate past; implications concern the present, the meaning right now of what just happened; and applications envision future considerations.

Formulate your own roster of questions for a particular exercise. I suggest doing this as follows. Read the suggested questions provided with the exercises detailed in the following pages. Then, without referring to the exercises in this book, make up your own questions, being sure that you are concentrating on the area or areas you believe most useful. Questions about what happened will always be on your list because they form a foundation for other sorts of questions.

In addition to developing an array of good debrief questions ahead of time, you should carefully think through your questioning strategy beforehand. This is essential if you are not sure how to orchestrate the debrief or have not done an exercise before. The key is to start the debrief with a good question about what occurred, then guide the discussion organically, with even flow, through to implications and applications. Assuredly, there is not a strict linear progression in a successful debrief from what happened to implications to applications. It may be desirable to trace one particular phenomenon from an exercise through all three before returning to the what happened part of another phenomenon. Only through practice can a facilitator acquire a sense of where to go next in a debrief and why.

It is especially important that you think very carefully about how you are going to lead a group into composing a collective portrait of what occurred in an activity. Understand that most people do not come by such behavior naturally. When you ask them what happened, initial responses may be superficial and simplistic, such as "We solved it" or "We worked together as a team"—to which I often respond, "Yes, but what did you do to solve it?" Be assured that patiently extracting from a group the step-by-step moves members took is not only useful prelude to further questioning but also important observational skill building. As to more advanced questions about implications and applications, you may choose to emphasize one over the other, or you may choose to give equal play to both.

Your roster of questions, when complete, will indicate clearly whether you are prepared to conduct a competent debrief. Furthermore, it will provide feedback to you on how well you have tailored the exercise to fit your particular objectives. The objectives ought to be transparent from a perusal of the questions. Finally, the questions can serve as a crude checklist for your observations as an activity unfolds.

Remember that whatever happens in an activity, there will be plenty to talk about in the debrief. Whatever the character and quality of interactions in an activity, participants will have had an experience, their own experience. The experience may have included familiar faces or unfamiliar ones. It may have come across as significantly different from experiences normally associated with professional development, or similar to others they have had. Whatever its degree of novelty, its character, and its texture, it will have power, and it will generate substantial mental energy on the part of participants that can be exploited in the debrief.

A successful debrief can start out slowly and unevenly and reach a crest toward the end, or it can take on momentum at the beginning, then trail off at the end. The job of the facilitator is to capitalize on the experience of the participants. For example, I once did an exercise with a group in which my first reaction was that they had made a real hash of the exercise. "How could they have done so poorly," I said to myself. The debrief afterward was one of the best I have ever led. This particular group learned more from its iteration of the exercise than any of the groups with which I had done it before, all of whom had done it "better."

The Order of the Exercises

There is a logic to the order of the exercises presented in each section. One progression is from introductory to more advanced, from exercises that provide a baseline perspective or are easier to orchestrate to ones that are more complex, multifaceted, and comprehensive. Another is whether an exercise offers more concrete and direct experience or calls on more abstract capacities. Finally, I placed toward the end of a list exercises that are slightly higher risk—for example, they deprive participants of sight, or they demand greater frankness or openness on the part of participants.

Following is a list of the exercises grouped by leadership and organizational development objective. The theme or purpose of each exercise is captured in the accompanying phrase.

Chapter 3, Focus on Risking Innovation

- **Spacejam:** When faced with increasing resource constraints, innovate!

- **Magic Steps:** Get from one place to another through innovative thinking and action.

- **Fishbowl Consultant:** Share responsibility for taking initiative and support others in doing the same.

- **Feedback Theater:** Cultivate imagination and confront the challenges of creative communication.

- **Innovation Maze:** Link leadership to followership and design support systems for risk takers.

- **Towering Vision:** Design, express, and sell creative vision.

Chapter 4, Focus on Fostering Collaboration

- **Concentric Conversations:** Shape common meaning by tapping everyone's point of view.

- **Working Norms:** Establish ground rules for the teamwork ahead.

- **Discussion Functions:** Make group discussions productive by fostering self-conscious participation.

- **Planning from the Ground Up:** Start small and build toward common points of view.

- **My Spot:** Honor individual perspective in team functioning.

- **Shaping the Future:** Envision effective working relationships in the face of unseen challenges.

- **Marking Effective Teamwork:** Codify practices that make accomplishing team tasks easier.

Chapter 5, Focus on Managing Conflict

- **Witch and Watch:** Unpack the confusion caused by crisscrossing communications.

- **Bureaucracy:** Experience hierarchy's effects on group problem solving.

- **Evacuation Drill:** See how scarce resources spiced with exigency affects group decision making.

- **Voices:** Elicit diverse opinions on key issues.

- **Tug of War:** Sharpen differences of opinion and air idiosyncratic approaches to defending them.

- **Leaders' Walk:** Pace off the tensions inherent in leadership-followership dynamics.

- **Ritual Conflict:** Reflect, and reflect on, the remarkably innocent origins of group conflict.

Chapter 6, Focus on Using Diversity

- **Mapping Diversity:** Understand the places that define colleagues' perspectives.

- **Diversity Bingo:** Distinguish both subjects and objects of stereotyping.

- **The Being:** Represent, and capitalize on, essential aspects of group diversity.

- **Listening in More Than One Voice:** Assume another persona for good listening and added perspective.

- **Stereotypes:** Watch stereotyping stymie the accomplishment of group task.

Each exercise description contains several sections:

- Purposes: The why of the exercise, especially its tie to a principal organizational objective

- Setup: What is needed to prepare for and do the activity

- Instructions: How to conduct the activity

- Success markers: Steps to take or signs to watch to ensure desired results

- Strategic considerations: Fitting the exercise into a sequence that makes for positive effect

- Questions about what happened, implications, and applications: Promising material for a sound debrief

Most of these activities I learned by experiencing them firsthand as a participant. A few of them I read about. Several I learned from a colleague or collaborated with a colleague to devise. I myself fashioned a handful of them. Virtually all of them I reshaped over time to meet my own or clients' special needs.

All the material relating to the exercises is my own composition. This includes linking the exercises to specific organizational objectives, intended purposes of the exercises, instructions for conducting activities and debriefs, insights into achieving or noting successful facilitation, strategic considerations, and exemplary debriefing questions.

Exercises on Risking Innovation

Introduction

Risking innovation, in two words, frames one of the most daunting challenges confronting contemporary organizational leaders. Interpreted together, the words speak to a need for marked self-consciousness and exceptional effort, essential ingredients for overcoming mental inertia within organizations. Organizational inertia grows under the weight of convention, is strengthened by a web of patterned behaviors that reinforce the status quo, and makes stepping out or acting against the grain an extraordinarily difficult thing to do—an even more difficult thing to encourage others to do. Inertia always lurks in the shadows as poor performance shows up in sharp relief.

At base, risking innovation involves the extemporaneous exercise of imagination, publicly exhibited. Such on-the-spot creativity, demonstrated in the company of one's peers, demands of the individual a combination of presence of mind, courage, and will. Hamlet's springs of action and Goethe's boldness having genius in it come to mind. That these ideas have prominence in great literature suggests that making them come alive in organizations requires thoughtful preparation and execution. Self-confidence regarding one's ideas, along with an ability to overcome the fear that others will discount them when they are offered up, are seeds that must be carefully nurtured. Hothouse environments may be the most appropriate places to begin this process before any flowering in the real world of organizational functioning can be expected.

The exercises that follow provide significant opportunities to practice the risking of innovation, both the summoning of will by individuals to express imaginative ideas and the struggle in groups to transform them into collective action. Among their number is a mix of the mild (Spacejam and Magic Steps), the modestly demanding (Feedback Theater and Fishbowl Consultant), and the more intense (Innovation Maze and Towering Vision). The first two offer a feel for the challenges of risking innovation, the second two pose problems that promote new ways of thinking and acting, and the last two demand considerable thought and deft interaction as well as calling into question standard operating procedures.

All the exercises are heavily interactive. All encourage creativity. All offer an arena that is foreign to the workplace of the participants. In the case of a mandate such as risking innovation, "foreign" offers substantial benefits, including

- aims that are highly generalized, not specific to a particular organization;

- artificial rules and constraints that beckon participants to test limits; and

- problems that require creative as opposed to rote thinking.

Together the conditions imposed by the exercises serve as an invitation for participants to exercise their imaginations in service to innovation in ways they would be unlikely to do so on the job. The debriefs of the exercises crystallize learning and point up numerous possibilities for doing things differently back in the workplace.

SPACEJAM

Purposes

This exercise is meant to convince a group that it has the capacity to innovate, to press the edge of the envelop with regard to the challenge it is facing. For participants, doing Spacejam feels a lot like doing Musical Chairs. What differentiates the two is that Spacejam promotes collaboration rather than competition, inclusion rather than exclusion, thoughtful shepherding of resources rather than forced expropriation of limited resources.

Setup

Props for the exercise include a number of rope slings of different diameter that can form circles on the floor. Rope the width of clothesline is best. Slings should vary from about a foot to a yard or more in diameter. The number of slings that will be necessary depends on the number of participants. A rough algorithm is a two-to-one ratio of people to slings. For 15 people, seven or eight slings will suffice. The smallest slings should be spacious enough to accommodate both feet of one adult standing. The largest should accommodate both feet of about 5 adults standing together, if the total number of participants is 15. The exercise normally consumes about a half hour in toto, including debrief.

Instructions

The facilitator begins by asking the participants to stand and introduces the exercise by making reference to contemporary challenges that compel groups to do more with less, to be innovative in the face of declining resources. Then the facilitator lays the full complement of rope slings out on the floor, with several feet between any two slings, and directs each participant to take up a stance inside a sling, any sling. Both feet of participants should be inside the sling. When participants are positioned as requested, the facilitator says that upon a signal from him or her, participants will have to move to another sling from the one they are presently in. Whichever sling they choose to move to, they must have both feet inside it. The group should also observe silence as the exercise proceeds.

For the first two switches, the facilitator merely issues a signal and does nothing else as participants move about. With the third switch, the facilitator moves quickly as participants are changing spots and removes two slings from play. Gradually, perhaps one sling at a time, the facilitator removes all but one sling, the largest one.

Success Markers

During one of the transitions prior to the elimination of all but one remaining sling, it usually dawns on a few participants that all of them will not be able to fit in the remaining slings without changing tactics. The constraints the exercise imposes gradually force a shift in the group's manner of doing things. This sometimes occurs haltingly, with some participants in the early going behaving as if the exercise were Musical Chairs. Eventually the group reaches a tacit consensus on how it has to behave to fit all participants into the one remaining rope circle. Substantial mirth usually accompanies the activity, and the solution of the problem incurs some mild self-congratulation.

You know you are likely to have a fruitful discussion if one participant makes a suggestion for dealing with the shortage of rope circles and others ignore him or her and go on cramming their erect bodies into fewer and fewer circumferences. Another positive sign is the emerging sense of satisfaction that spreads through a group when a breakthrough innovation develops and all go along with it. Although neither of these two need occur for a rich debrief, they are nonetheless positive indications.

Strategic Considerations

Spacejam is an excellent example of an exercise that some might view as an inconsequential ice breaker, an experience that loosens people up but has little real point to it. I include it here to substantiate a major contention of this book. Even the most mild experiences, many reminiscent of children's games, can inform people's bodies and minds of consequential inclinations. These will stand them in good stead when, in their organizations, the stakes are much higher, yet the challenges are very similar to the ones they faced in the exercise.

The exercise can be done at any point in the evolution of group work. If the choice is to do it early on, the facilitator should have reason to believe that the group will welcome, rather than reject as silly, the proposition that it might benefit from child's play. The facilitator could suffer an unfortunate loss of credibility if the latter were the case. If the choice is to insert it later on, the exercise will likely offer mild yet meaningful diversion from intense interactions, carrying with it some positive reinforcement for innovative thinking.

The debrief of Spacejam should be crisply brief.

Questions About What Happened

+ What did you as a group do to solve the problem you faced?

+ Who did what to lead you to the solution?

+ What was the process by which innovation was proposed and adopted by the group? Was a solution proposed and adopted readily? Was it resisted at first? Was it adopted explicitly or tacitly? By all at once, or by a lead group followed by all?

Questions About Implications and Applications

+ What are the implications for your work together, specifically for your adoption of innovative proposals, and for the relationship between those in your group who propose innovations and those who adopt them?

+ What does your behavior in the exercise tell you about the challenges you face in achieving a balance between competition and collaboration?

+ Can you think of potential solutions you might craft to attain the balance you want?

+ What other lessons are there to be drawn from the exercise regarding group decision making?

+ What was the source of the joy for you in this exercise, and in what ways might you replicate it in your work with each other?

MAGIC STEPS

Purposes

This exercise provides a group with convincing evidence that "getting from here to there" is not as easy as it appears. Innovative thinking and action are essential to high performance, and at times spring from unlikely sources. The bedrock of innovation is novel ideas. Spurring idea origination, listening carefully as colleagues tentatively advance ideas, and ensuring that ideas take hold on behavior are significant challenges for groups and organizations. Leaders are perpetually seeking ways to convince those they work with that their impulses toward innovation will be honored and supported. Magic Steps aims to help in this regard.

Setup

To prepare for the exercise, the facilitator must locate an appropriate space and craft a set of "magic steps." These can be made from inexpensive materials such as pliable plastic place mats or sturdy pieces of cardboard. For a working group of 20 people, approximately 12 steps will suffice. Among the 12, about half should be large enough for two people to step on at once, albeit in close, uncomfortable quarters. The other half should be smaller, large enough for only one person to stand on at a time.

The best space in which to conduct the exercise is a hallway or similarly bounded space, wide enough for about half a dozen people to walk abreast. For a group of 20, the facilitator should mark off an unobstructed stretch between 30 and 40 feet in length along the hallway. The exercise normally consumes about an hour, including debrief. Illustration 3.1 shows how participants and steps might be configured as the activity begins to unfold.

Instructions

The facilitator gathers the group at one end of the stretch and designates that place as the start. The facilitator states that the challenge is for all group members to reach the other end safely. Putting them at risk is the fact that the area between the start and finish is a mire of highly toxic material from which only magic steps can protect them. By placing the steps along the path and walking on them, the group will be able to traverse this dangerous terrain. The hitch is that if a

Illustration 3.1.

step, when in use on the mire, is not continuously in contact with a body part of one of the members of the group, it will instantaneously disappear into the mire and be lost forever as a resource to the group. To illustrate, imagine a step placed on the mire that is left unattended for one microsecond as a group member jumps to another well-placed step. IT IS LOST, NO LONGER AVAILABLE! The facilitator removes it from play.

The facilitator carefully hands the set of magic steps to one of the members of the group and beckons them to get started. Although a time limit is not necessary, it may be desirable. If a time limit is imposed, it certainly will cause a sense of urgency and consequently less vigilant caretaking of the steps while in play.

Success Markers

Normally a group quickly caucuses. Various suggestions are put forth. One or two take hold. Many are ignored. The group moves swiftly to implement a strategy hastily developed. Perhaps it involves stringing members out across the mire using the steps, with a long-legged person taking the lead on the span. Inevitably, there are lapses in concentration and steps are lost. These losses capture the attention of the group, amplifying the enthusiasm of several who might have been on the verge of losing interest and concentration. The result is often regrouping, brief but intense discussion with a lot of ideas bandied about, and a revised strategy. Anything that resembles the above sequence usually leads to a productive debrief.

Strategic Considerations

Because the exercise is straight-out fun with almost no threatening aspects such as unsightedness or the handling of tough issues, it can be done at any point in the life cycle of a group's work. Yet because the main purpose is to instill impulses toward innovation and risk taking, it is best done after a group has charted a course, that is, established a vision and determined a strategy. The lessons of the exercise center on the sorts of capacities a group needs to accomplish something once it sets out on a course. It is desirable, therefore, for most members of the group to have a clear sense of what that something entails.

Questions About What Happened

✦ What was your group's strategy for tackling the challenge presented in the exercise? How did you arrive at this strategy? Where did the ideas that underlay it come from? Which of you had good ideas for proceeding? Were there ideas voiced that the group did not adopt?

✦ How did it happen that some ideas were adopted and others rejected? Did you have a system for uncovering ideas and incorporating them into the overall group strategy? Even if a system per se was never discussed, was one tacitly agreed to?

✦ Who played which roles in execution and what did they do? While they were executing, what did the rest of the group do?

✦ What happened when you lost magic step(s)? Did you revise your strategy or stay with your original game plan?

Questions About Implications

✦ Upon reflection, are there things you would have done differently? In terms of strategy? In terms of systems development? In terms of execution?

✦ Were you satisfied with the relative weight you gave to strategizing, to systems development and to execution? Would the balance you effected hold up well in a real organizational context? Why? Could you cite some examples?

✦ What are the parallels between losing magic steps and real losses that occur in organizations? What in your view do magic steps stand for?

✦ What about your reactions to the loss of magic steps? Are there any parallels here with reactions that would likely occur in real organizations?

Questions About Applications

✦ Are there maneuvers, analogous to ones you learned in this exercise, that you ought to incorporate into your group work? Which ones, for example, might help you fulfill your vision or implement your strategy?

✦ Exactly how are you going to go about adding these new capacities to those your group presently relies on? In particular, how are you going to get everybody from one point to another over difficult terrain, terrain that is likely to demand risk taking in the face of considerable constraint and diminished resources?

✦ Taking risks often results in loss rather than gain. How will you ensure that your fear of loss does not inhibit taking risks?

FISHBOWL CONSULTANT

Purposes

Distributing responsibility for initiative taking to all staff is one of the more daunting challenges confronting people in leadership positions. In hierarchic organizations, the positional leader, the person with a title by his or her name, is normally the one to spur innovative thinking and action within a work group. This exercise puts group members themselves squarely in charge of prompting their peers to take more risks in the way they address problems, rather than leaving that responsibility to the designated leader alone. Its purpose is to create a climate in which everyone in the group has an obligation not only to bring his or her own best ideas forth but to urge and assist fellow group members to do the same.

Setup

The exercise requires no props, just enough meeting space for groups of five or six people to sit in small circles while an equal number of their colleagues stand behind them. The net effect is that each person who is seated has one person standing right behind. Random assignment of participants is usually satisfactory, unless there is a reason for selective grouping.

One work unit in the exercise comprises 10 or 12 people, 5 or 6 standing close behind the 5 or 6 sitting. Illustration 3.2 depicts the appropriate configuration.

Well before the group convenes, the facilitator frames an issue or problem that needs addressing. It is important that the outcome of the group's deliberations on this topic be consequential, that top management not already have formulated a position that it wants the group to ratify. The exercise is particularly fit for the core concern a group faces, that which represents the very heart of its work together. Including debrief, the exercise takes about an hour.

Instructions

With participants in place, the facilitator states, in a succinct sentence or two, the issue or problem to be addressed and asks those who are seated to begin discussing it. The facilitator tells them that they will only have about 7 minutes to do so, and that the participants standing behind them are to serve as their consultants. The consultants' role is

Illustration 3.2.

to assist their clients in becoming effective contributors to the discussion. Consultants may not participate directly in the discussion. They can only communicate one-on-one with their clients.

After 7 minutes, the facilitator asks the participants to pause and tells the consultant-client duos to move away from the discussion circle and caucus with each other for about 3 minutes. The aim of these multiple *tête à tête's* is for consultants to assist their clients in boosting their contributions to the discussion, both the substance being addressed and the vigor and imagination being applied. The facilitator can easily egg them on by suggesting that the discussion could benefit from even more innovative thinking. After a few minutes, the facilitator calls the discussants and their consultants back to the circle and asks the discussants to embark on another 7- to 10-minute discussion.

When this second round is concluded, the facilitator requests a report from each group on the ideas it has come up with and records these on newsprint sheets. Abruptly, the facilitator asks participants to reverse roles: the consultants to sit down and become discussants, and the discussants to stand up and become consultants. Participants address the same topic and go through the same steps they just completed in their former roles—short discussion, brief caucus, short discussion.

In sum, the hour set aside for the exercise includes two 7-minute assisted discussions and two short caucuses for all participants, as well as time for the total group to summarize and the facilitator to record the results of the discussions. It also includes time for the whole group to review the sum total of its work and decide which pieces have the most promise for addressing the issue that is in front of them. At the very close, the facilitator conducts a relatively short debrief of the exercise to be sure that group members have identified novel ways to glean the innovative thinking of all group members as their work proceeds.

Success Markers

It is a promising development if the first caucuses between discussants and consultants are lively and enthusiastic. It is more promising yet if the caucuses provoke more intense and focused discussion than that which took place in the first rounds of discussion. The facilitator can influence the course of events by challenging the participants to be bolder and by recapping their previous discussions in ways that push for greater breadth and depth of treatment by participants.

Strategic Considerations

As already noted, this exercise can be quite fruitful if a group is ready to confront core issues and if a facilitator can frame and reframe the group's initial formulations clearly and succinctly. Group readiness is present when two conditions apply: The group has attained a common understanding of the most significant issues before it, and group members have achieved a degree of mutual comfort that allows them to challenge each other's thinking without fear of causing offense. In sum, the exercise, to be most effective, should be done with a group that has worked together for a while and is ready to advance to a higher level of effectiveness.

Questions About What Happened

- ✦ What was it like to be a consultant? To be a client?

- ✦ Describe what happened in the client-consultant caucuses. What seemed to be helpful? What was not so helpful?

- ✦ What were the differences between the two distinct discussions you had while in the role of discussant? Substantive differences? Differences in intensity, tone, approach?

Questions About Implications

- ✦ Did the hour you dedicated to the exercise produce any useful material for dealing with the substantive problems you face? Why so or why not?

- ✦ What is the value added in having a personal consultant, if any? What is the value added in acting as a consultant to a colleague, if any?

- ✦ Might these two roles be more of an expected norm in group work? Why so or not?

- ✦ What if all group members were simultaneously consultant and client to all others? What might such an arrangement look like, feel like? Would it work at all, or just result in chaos?

Questions About Applications

- ✦ Given the experience of Fishbowl Consultant, are there aspects of it that you should consider fitting into your broadening portfolio of teamwork skills? Specifically, what should you be doing differently with regard to managing your group's dynamics? Are there particular areas of individual skill development that experiencing this exercise calls to mind?

FEEDBACK THEATER

Purposes

Feedback Theater is an exercise about creativity, communication, and collaboration. It offers participants insight into how these essential ingredients of organizational effectiveness interact for positive effect. It also sheds light on the nuances that make these a genuine challenge for people with leadership aspirations.

Setup

The exercise requires no equipment or aids of any sort. It can be accomplished in almost any work space as long as there are separate spaces for small groups to talk and develop plans out of sight of other small groups with whom they will interact as the exercise progresses. Including debrief, the exercise normally consumes about an hour.

Instructions

The facilitator divides all in the room into groups of six, and further asks these groups to subdivide into two subgroups of three each. The facilitator tells participants that the task to be performed will be the responsibility of the group of six as a whole, but that the two subgroups will engage in different functions to accomplish that task. The composition of groups and subgroups can be either random or preset. In my own experience, random groups suffice for most purposes.

The task is for one subgroup of three to replicate with total accuracy a visual representation that its counterpart subgroup has devised while out of sight. For ease of understanding, let me assign designations to the two subgroups. Subgroup A—three people—is the design group; subgroup B—three people—is the implementation group. A goes to a separate work space, out of sight of B, to develop a representation or sign using only group members' bodies as artistic materials.

In effect, subgroup A composes a living snapshot of a set of ideas. These ideas may be in reaction to a thematic prompt offered by the facilitator. Alternatively, the participants may be allowed to choose themes themselves. Either way, all three members of subgroup A need to represent the same sign. Thus, there will be three identical body molds of one common sign, not three different body molds making up one composite sign. For example, all three members of A display themselves as nonwelcoming Statues of Liberty, all three looking exactly alike. Normally, subgroup A should take no more than 10 to 15 minutes to do its design work.

When subgroup A has its sign ready, it returns to the room where subgroup B has remained in its absence. The members of A must now teach the members of B the sign they have concocted. However—and it's a big caveat—members of A may not show members of B their sign. Subgroup B must "act it out," that is, attempt various moves and configurations without knowing anything at all about the design subgroup A wants it to replicate, except perhaps the theme it suggests. For their part, members of A can only cue members of B by signaling yes, no, or maybe—thumbs up, thumbs down, or flat palm, for example—as subgroup B struggles to produce the unknown sign. Illustration 3.3 captures essential aspects of the scenario.

Whether the facilitator specifies a theme for the sign making or not, the designers should be encouraged to be as free thinking and creative as they can. Yet subgroup A should understand that it will have to teach the sign it decides to subgroup B when it returns to the room. For its part, subgroup B should strategize how it might best weather the rigors of producing a sign that it has not seen. Its challenge is to be effective learners despite the obvious constraints.

It is difficult to specify particular themes that work well in this exercise. The main determinant should be the objectives the facilitator is attempting to achieve. In the early stages of working with a group, I often use themes that emphasize capacities I want to reinforce, such as collaborative decision making. Later on, I am more likely to choose themes that relate to the substance of the group's task. I once asked a group of educators to represent the notion of a community of learners in its sign.

The facilitator must also decide beforehand whether to explain to both subgroups the constraints that will govern their interactions when they come together to complete the task. One option is to leave the constraints vague, saying only that subgroup A will not be able to show its sign to B. I prefer saying as little as possible. It makes for more authentic and spontaneous reactions on everyone's part. On the other hand, being explicit about the constraints does lay out the challenges before the participants and encourages them to plan how to deal with them.

Normally, subgroup A can "teach" its sign to B in about 10 to 15 minutes. It may take longer, however, if subgroup A comes up with a very complicated configuration full of nuances, such as hands placed at particular angles and fingers deployed in special ways. Time may

Illustration 3.3.

also be extended if subgroup A fails to understand that B, faced with severe communication restrictions, will likely be trying to alight on simple notions or ones reminiscent of configurations that might make instantaneous sense. If subgroup B, for its part, does not work out a simple learning system by which it can receive the messages A conveys, the exercise can become protracted. One such system could involve each member of B focusing solely on the actions of a counterpart member of A.

Success Markers

Feedback Theater usually promotes considerable gaiety within participant groups, the same sort that is generated in a game of Charades. Facilitators should remain confident that frivolity will not diminish the potential for learning in the exercise. Beside the fun, there is likely to be substantial frustration for both designers and implementers because of the constraints on open communication between them. Implementers will undoubtedly struggle with how much bodily ingenuity to display to attain the right answer, designers with how to provide coherent guidance to implementers. All the above is good grist for discussion afterward.

Strategic Considerations

Feedback Theater is not a particularly good opener, nor is it an effective culminating experience. Rather, it fits somewhere in the middle of a set of learning experiences. To have the desired effects, the exercise requires a certain amount of ease, even trust, among participants. They must loosen up, be creative, even be willing to look a little foolish in the presence of colleagues. Because the emphases include creativity and collaboration, the exercise works best when, in the judgment of the facilitator, the group is open to learning from folly.

Questions About What Happened

✦ What did you do as designers to create a representation? How did this process unfold? What steps did you take to develop a concept and represent it?

✦ As teachers, what did you do to prepare for the teaching you were about to undertake? Were there any special things you talked about doing with the learners when you reconvened with them? Anything that took into account the constraints the learners/implementers might be facing?

✦ As learners/implementers, what did you do to prepare to execute effectively the representation developed by the designers? What learning devices or systems did you develop?

✦ What sorts of things did you actually do in the heat of the action as learners/implementers to grasp the ideas the designers/teachers were trying to get across?

✦ As designers/teachers, what did you do to get across your ideas to the learner/implementers?

✦ Did either of the subgroups devise and execute workable systems on the spot? How about systems that seemed workable in theory, but turned out not to be functional when brought into play?

Questions About Implications

✦ What sorts of things worked for you, either in the preparation stage or in the execution stage?

✦ Why, from your point of view, did one or another thing work, or not?

✦ What do you take away from this exercise in terms of a better understanding of teaching and learning in general? Are there implications here for what a learning organization is all about?

✦ What sorts of things do you take away from this exercise in terms of the relationship between planning and implementation in organizational contexts?

✦ What did you learn from this exercise about creativity? About taking risks? About the value of making a fool of yourself? About making mistakes and getting back to the task at hand afterward?

✦ What did you learn about creativity, not only the creativity involved in using a completely different medium to capture themes but the creativity involved in effective teaching and learning?

Questions About Applications

✦ With what is in your minds—and your bodies—right now in the wake of this exercise, what can you distill from this exercise that is worth adapting to your work context?

✦ Can you cite instances from last week, or anticipated ones from the upcoming week, in which the sorts of creativity demonstrated in the exercise might usefully be put into play?

✦ How about situations where you might apply some of what you just learned about the requisites of fit communication for teaching and learning?

✦ How about venues where you might apply some of what you just learned about a more desirable relationship between planning and implementation in your organization?

✦ What lessons have you gleaned about some of the subtle—or not so subtle—requisites of collaboration in organizations? How might they be applied to your work context?

INNOVATION MAZE

Purposes

This exercise demonstrates that aggressive followership is as potent a form of leadership as more traditional forms. More specifically it shows that

- solid support of an innovator by colleagues is as integral to leadership as an innovator braving uncertainties on the frontier of action;

- making mistakes is essential to organizational growth and effectiveness, as long as systems are developed to avoid making the same mistake twice; and

- elemental forms of group intelligence and systems thinking are often the most appropriate means of overcoming organizational challenges.

Setup

Before the group arrives, the facilitator sets up the maze as shown in Illustration 3.4 and Diagram 3.1. With 1-inch-wide masking tape, the facilitator lays down a 6-square-by-9-square grid on the floor or pavement. The squares should have roughly 18-inch sides.

Illustration 3.4.

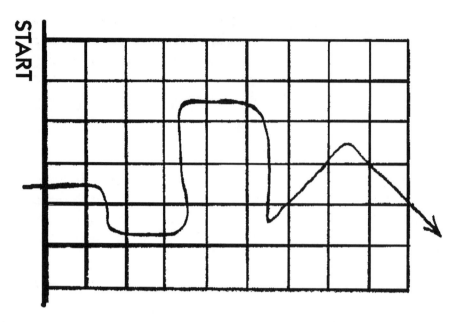

Diagram 3.1.

It usually takes about an hour and a half to complete the exercise, sometimes more if the debrief stretches into lengthy treatment of applications.

Instructions

The facilitator begins by asking 12 to 25 participants to stand up and cluster behind the start line. The facilitator first explains succinctly the purpose and aim of the exercise. For example, "This is a group problem-solving exercise about leadership and followership and the mutual support that is required for teamwork. Your aim is to get all group members through the maze by following a single path or line that is formed by adjacent squares." Then the facilitator clarifies, saying that the path begins with one of the squares in row 1 and proceeds—in a curved, not a straight, line—through row 9, after which a person exits the maze. The facilitator further states that only he or she has the key that depicts the correct path through the maze. Diagram 3.1 exemplifies such a key. A set time will be allowed for both planning and implementation, usually 17 minutes for a group of about 20.

The facilitator reminds the group again that the right path is one continuous line made up of adjacent or contiguous squares. The facilitator also tells participants the key constraints or rules that will govern their actions as they go about solving the problem. The facilitator ends by stating, somewhat tongue in cheek, that participants will be awarded $1 million if they get through the maze in the time allotted; however, they will be assessed a $100,000 penalty for each rule violation. Following are the rules and associated penalties as appropriate:

- Only one person at a time is allowed on the maze.

- If a person steps on a wrong square, he or she will be "buzzed" and must withdraw from the maze. There is no penalty for being buzzed. To withdraw successfully, however, a person must follow the exact same path used to get in. If he or she fails to do so, a penalty will be assessed.

- Establishing a rotation of "innovators" attempting the maze is required, that is, once one group member is buzzed off the maze, another tries, and so on.

- No "Hansel and Gretel," that is, leaving a trail of crumbs on the maze for others to follow.

- No sketching on paper or blackboards, that is, no diagramming the unfolding path as it is discovered.

- When in a planning mode, the entire group must be behind the start line, and talking is allowed. When implementing, that is, an "innovator" is on the maze, group members may array them- selves in any way they choose around the maze, but talking is not allowed. (Not calling attention to the possibility, the facilitator can suggest that there is nothing to prevent a group from planning for a short time, then trying out an approach on the maze, then returning behind the line to refine its plans.) A penalty will be assessed for violating this rule, that is, talking while executing.

- When an innovator is out on the maze, none of his or her fellow members, arrayed around the maze, may touch the maze with any part of his or her body. A penalty will be assessed for violating this rule.

The exercise has greater effect if the group fails on its first try to get through the maze, that is, in the first time allotment. The facilitator can manufacture this failure by carefully fitting the amount of time allowed and the difficulty of the path through the maze to the size and composition of the group. It is usually not possible, for example, for a group of 20 adults to get through the maze on its first try if it has only 15 to 17 minutes to do it and there is at least one backtracking move in the path. By backtracking move, I mean that the next correct square on the grid is behind or diagonally behind the innovator rather than to his or her side or ahead of him or her.

Generally, the larger the group, the more difficulty it will have; a large group will likely consume more time agreeing on a plan of action. The more young people there are in a group, the more quickly the group will get the first person through the maze, however; this is attributable, I speculate, to youth's greater penchant to throw caution to the wind and make mistakes willy-nilly. If there is a backtracking move in the path, this will cause some holdup for most groups. Forward movement is naturally sought, or intuitively seen as correct, especially with the arrows on the floor pointing that way.

Following a group's failed attempt on its first try, the facilitator conducts a relatively short discussion—perhaps 10 to 15 minutes—to elicit participants' initial reactions to being on the maze, their perspectives on the best resources available to them for problem solving, and their suggestions for improved performance. (See the suggested questions below.) Toward the end of this short debrief, the facilitator says something such as, "So if you had another shot at this, what would you do differently?" After listening to, and perhaps summarizing, several suggestions that individuals offer, the facilitator says, "Well, I will give you one more shot—slightly less time, different path through the maze." Then the group makes its second and final attempt based on what it learned from its first try.

Success Markers

Much depends on the facilitator's making good projections. The facilitator has to make an intuitive assessment of the group's capabilities, hoping that it will get one of its members two thirds to three quarters of the way through the maze before time runs out. It is not a significant liability to learning if a group actually gets one of its members all the way through on its first try yet is unable to get all its members through. It is somewhat inhibiting if a group makes only very slight progress on the maze or doesn't step out on it at all.

Whatever occurs, it is important to remember that there will be much to discuss. Although I have never had a group fail to get a person on the maze at all in its first try, it would make for an interesting debrief nonetheless. I have also had groups prevail despite my best efforts to have them fail on their first try. Although there may some downside here for learning, there is still the potential for a rich debrief.

If a group fails the first time through, its collective motivation level will likely soar on its second attempt. This is usually evidenced in the vigorous discussion that takes place before the group sets out on the maze and the universal participation of group members in support roles around the maze. The emotional intensity is often palpable on a group's second try, whereas on the first there may have been more watchers than doers.

Strategic Considerations

This exercise works best when a group is about to undertake an important collective effort in which mutual support by all group members is essential. It can have profound and long-lasting effects when participants are about to proceed with colleagues into unfamiliar territory in pursuit of a shared objective. The exercise does not serve well as an initial experience for a group just getting underway, nor as a culminating event to top off and build on a success. Prior investment in shaping effective working relationships among group members is essential for the lessons of this exercise to take hold.

A successful debrief of the maze can be accomplished in about 15 to 20 minutes for Round 1 and up to 45 minutes for Round 2.

Questions for Round 1

+ What was it like to be out on the maze trying to discover the correct path?

+ What was the penalty for making a mistake, that is, stepping on the wrong square? If there was no explicit penalty for making a mistake, why did innovators hesitate, mulling over which square to choose next? What was going on in the heads of the innovators?

+ Which actions by your fellow group members helped you as an innovator make headway? Which hindered? Were you getting clear signals on which square to step next?

+ What emphasis did your group give to planning as opposed to execution? Were the balance and interaction between the two as you like them? Did they work well for you?

+ Did you have an explicit group strategy for getting through the maze? Describe it. Which parts of your strategy worked well for you? Which did not?

+ What was your strategy to support the person who was out on the maze? How well did your support strategy work?

+ What other things worked for you?

+ What might you do differently next time, if you had another shot at getting the group through the maze?

Questions for Round 2

+ What did you do differently the second time around? Did you change any of your tactics? Why? Which tactics worked for you; which did not?

+ Identify the major innovations that contributed to your successful completion of the exercise. Who authored these innovations? Which were attributable to individuals, which to support groups?

+ There seemed to be a noticeable increase in group intensity and concentration on your second try. Fewer members were disengaged, or only marginally engaged. Why?

+ Did your group abide by all the rules? How come? Did you, individually or collectively, decide to break some? How come?

+ What was the essential task or tasks involved in this exercise? Beyond the obvious one of getting all members through the maze on the correct path, what was this exercise all about?

+ What are the lessons of Innovation Maze for how leaders should behave in organizations? Listen for and reinforce such lessons as support for making mistakes; quickly developing systems to learn from mistakes so as not to make the same ones twice; designing, developing, and effecting support systems for innovators; and letting group intelligence prevail over individual intelligence on tasks that lend themselves to such an approach.

+ What does this exercise tell you about leadership? Will you reshape your working definition of leadership in light of the experience you just had?

+ Can you identify a recent instance where the lessons of this exercise, if applied in your organization, would have had a positive effect on performance?

+ Can you identify a situation on the horizon in which it will really make a difference to quality and productivity if the lessons are applied?

TOWERING VISION

Purposes

Towering Vision presents a wide range of opportunities for organizational development. Any or all of the following can be explored in great depth in the wake of completing the activity:

- The role of visioning in organizations

- Key dimensions of effective teamwork such as role differentiation and mutual support

- The linking of individual creative capacities with team creative capacities

- The relationship of design to execution in organizational functioning

- The interplay of planning and implementation

- The ways in which competition among groups can detract from effective execution, especially when a group fails to agree on solid design criteria and hold to them as implementation gets underway

- The relationship between substantive ideas and promotional images and the ethics of fair competition

Setup

Equipment and space needs for Towering Vision are as follows: round tables for several groups of six to eight to confer; nearby each table, ample floor space for the construction of a paper tower that may be taller than the participants when standing up. Each work group needs a stack of newspapers about 6 inches thick, a small ball of twine or string, and a pair of scissors. About an hour and a half should be set aside for the exercise, including debrief.

In preparation for doing the exercise, the facilitator has to make two important decisions. First is whether to ask the participants to build structures that represent a certain theme. In one instance, for example, I asked a large group aiming to develop a strategy for improved land use planning to build structures that represented the modes of collaboration necessary for an effective strategy. In another, I instructed participants to build structures that represented essential aspects of principled leadership, based on the reading we had done on the topic together.

There may be enough yield from the exercise without the existence of a thematic prompt, however. In a number of instances, I provided no theme for a group, relying instead on the considerable potential of the exercise for organizational learning in general. Experience itself is likely to be the best guide for facilitators here. Try the exercise both with and without a theme and acquire a feel for what works with different groups under varying conditions and contexts.

The second decision is whether to administer a leadership assessment or inventory to the participants in conjunction with the exercise. The way this works is that participants complete a questionnaire, and the results are scored and data are aggregated before they begin the exercise itself. Because the assessment chosen affects the content and direction of the discussion following the activity, the facilitator has to be quite self-conscious about objectives. If, for example, the facilitator chooses to administer a Myers-Briggs-type assessment—which generates personality-specific information—then the debrief will be replete with references to participants' personal attributes.

For my part, I have shied away from assessments that focus on individual attributes. Towering Vision is a powerful enough experience without factoring in the sometimes volatile reactions that can accompany personality inventories. Instead, I prefer assessments that uncover participants' preferences and priorities. I have, for example, done the exercise in the context of the results from a questionnaire a colleague and I developed on collaborative leadership capabilities. We based it on attributes described in *The Leadership Challenge* by Kouzes and Posner (1991). The instrument and instructions for its use appear at the end of this exercise as Chart 3.1.

For a group of insurance executives seeking to improve their team leadership skills, Towering Vision, experienced in the wake of the assessment we prepared, engendered significant insights into the dynamics of their approach to collaborative leadership. The results provoked hearty discussion of task and result orientation versus relationship and process orientation. Because we had administered the questionnaire to both the executives with whom we were working and their supervisors, we were able to discuss not only the leadership inclinations of the participants but also how they compared to those of their supervisors.

Instructions

These instructions are adapted from a worksheet developed in 1993 by Blue Ridge Resource Group. The facilitator begins by asking participants to divide into work groups of about six to eight. Because the exercise involves competition among groups and ends with preferential voting among completed structures, it works best when there are three or more work groups. After distributing the materials as listed above to each group, the facilitator states that the challenge is to design and build a towerlike structure with the materials provided, and only those provided. The structure must be self-standing on the floor, with nothing propping it up such as string tied to furniture.

When completed, the structures will be judged. Quality of concept, creativity of design, structural stability, and height are the main bases for judgment, and each group can decide for itself which ones to emphasize.

The facilitator notes that there are timed steps for proceeding with design and construction. There is limited time at the outset—5 to 7 minutes—for individuals to think about the structure they would like to see built and sketch their ideas on paper. After this brief period, each work group has about 15 minutes to discuss its design ideas and arrive at one integrated design. There will then be a period of 20 to 25 minutes for construction. Toward the end of this phase, groups should begin discussing how they will promote or sell their final product to their counterpart groups. An additional 15 minutes will be available for the groups to complete their promotional pitches and put other finishing touches on their work. It should be noted that the time allotments for each of these functions is flexible. Groups, in effect, have about an hour for design, construction, and marketing.

When ready to present, each group can take up to 5 minutes to showcase its product for others in the room. After the presentations, each group casts one vote for the structure that best meets the criteria stated at the outset. Groups may not vote for their own structure.

The debrief of the exercise can take as little as half an hour, although it can go on fruitfully for an hour or more. If done in conjunction with a leadership assessment of the participants, the debrief can be quite extensive, particularly the segment that relates to applications to a particular context.

Success Markers

Enthusiasm and intense engagement on the part of participants are the two surest signs that the activity will lead to a productive debrief. It is also helpful if the separate work groups show signs of open competition with one another. For example, one group might deviate from its original design so that its structure attains a height greater than that of its neighbor, or another might adopt a design wrinkle pioneered by someone else. Finally, there are seeds of success in the camaraderie that develops in each work group and the humor, sometimes outright belly laughter, generated in the naming and selling of the final products.

Strategic Considerations

Towering Vision can be an excellent capstone experience, allowing a group to demonstrate an array of skills that members have been perfecting over some time. Done in the context of a theme and accompanied by a leadership assessment, the exercise can offer complex issues for discussion. Implications of what happened and applications of lessons learned can be elaborate. Altered individual and group behavior under these circumstances will require considerable reinforcement and follow-up. Alternatively, the exercise fares equally well as a vehicle for diagnosis. It provides a group that is just getting underway with a host of areas it can work on and skills it can shore up.

Questions About What Happened

+ How did you divide your allotted time between individual and group design?

+ Did you establish different roles for each group member, for example, designer, folder or roller, promotional specialist?

+ How did your group decide on one design from among the several put forth by individuals? Was there contention or easy consensus?

+ Through the execution phase, did you stick with the design you chose, or adapt it as you saw what others were up to? Did you, in other words, engage in any form of "industrial espionage"?

+ Did your group do all the tasks—individual design, group design, group execution, group promotion—one after the other? Or was there overlap among the tasks?

+ Was there in effect strategic voting on the part of some groups or did your group vote its conscience? How paramount were the criteria in deciding which structure your group would vote for? Did one or more of the criteria dominate in your decision making?

+ Which criterion or criteria played the largest part in your thinking as you designed and built your structure?

+ What other things worked for you, which did not?

Questions About Implications

+ Did the way you allocated time for design as against implementation work for you? Why?

+ Did the roles your group established meet the expectations you had for them?

+ If your group altered its design as the building process unfolded, what were the advantages and disadvantages of doing this?

+ What are lessons of this exercise for team functioning in organizations, for example, about the relationship and balance between design functions and implementation functions, building a durable base for operations that can withstand unanticipated pressures, deploying group members' gifts strategically, the value of agreed-on criteria for evaluating performance and product, the critical role of imagination, the careful allocation of time to different of tasks, and the relationship between followership and leadership?

Questions About Applications

+ What kind of "structure" is your group building in your organization, that is, what sort of vision are you shaping? Is it well thought through and conceptually strong?

+ What will you do to ensure that your structure is lofty and yet has a firm base?

+ What are your criteria for judging this structure as you design it; how will you hold to them as you proceed—what systems of quality control will you to put into place?

+ How will you distribute individual assignments as you set about your common task?

+ Which of your group will be working on marketing your structure?

+ To whom will you market it, that is, whom do you have to convince to buy this structure, and how will you get them to do so?

CHART 3.1. Collaborative Leadership Qualities Inventory

Below is a list of leadership traits. Rate the importance of these traits to effective leaders seeking to create high performance organizations. Use the following scale: 1 = of little importance; 2 = of modest importance; 3 = of marked importance; 4 = of great importance. Your number total cannot exceed 60 and you must show at least five 1s and five 4s in your tally.

1. Question assumptions underlying current practices.	1 2 3 4
2. Formulate solutions with an eye to current political and organizational dynamics.	1 2 3 4
3. Communicate effectively across the organization's departmental boundaries.	1 2 3 4
4. Have in-depth knowledge of a range of financial operations.	1 2 3 4
5. Attend to colleagues' aspirations for personal learning and development.	1 2 3 4
6. Listen to and incorporate diverse perspectives into decision making.	1 2 3 4
7. Engender the commitment of others to common goals.	1 2 3 4
8. Run meetings and make presentations effectively.	1 2 3 4
9. Communicate with customers to learn what they think.	1 2 3 4
10. Draw out others' personal preferences to search for common ground.	1 2 3 4
11. Surface conflicts before they become serious roadblocks.	1 2 3 4
12. Articulate a clear vision for how individuals might work more closely together.	1 2 3 4
13. Generate creative solutions in the midst of chaotic circumstances.	1 2 3 4
14. Show honesty and forthrightness in dealings with others.	1 2 3 4

15. Demonstrate a caring attitude toward others.	1	2	3	4
16. Shape working norms to include all cultural and ethnic groups in the workplace.	1	2	3	4
17. Shepherd financial resources to serve organizational objectives.	1	2	3	4
18. Seek representation of stakeholders in discussions that affect them.	1	2	3	4
19. Not only take risks, but encourage others to do the same.	1	2	3	4
20. Exhibit a sense of humor.	1	2	3	4
21. Demonstrate flexibility in responding to tough issues.	1	2	3	4
22. Build consensus among stakeholders on the direction of future operations.	1	2	3	4
23. Consistently build on others' ideas in problem-solving discussions.	1	2	3	4
24. Step in and redirect destructive conflict.	1	2	3	4
25. Promote recognition of others' contributions.	1	2	3	4

To generate a report, the facilitator tallies participants' responses as follows:

1, 6, 11, 16, 21 = Subtotal for challenging the process

2, 7, 12, 17, 22 = Subtotal for inspiring a shared vision

3, 8, 13, 18, 23 = Subtotal for enabling others to act

4, 9, 14, 19, 24 = Subtotal for modeling the way

5, 10, 15, 20, 25 = Subtotal for encouraging the heart

The subtotals should reflect a range, from highest to lowest priority, for the five different capacities. The facilitator then adds together the subtotals for the different groups of individuals for whom a tally should be reported, including the group as whole. This will provide a basis for useful comparisons.

See Kouzes & Posner (1991), pp. 7-13, for further elaboration of the five collaborative leadership capacities listed above. If it is possible to secure responses from more than one group of leaders with a reporting relationship to each other—such as managers of communications on the one hand and their top supervisors on the other—the debrief will be even more fruitful.

Exercises on Fostering Collaboration

Introduction

Collaboration comes in many forms, but teamwork may be its purest iteration. Building teams involves getting a group to act as if it were one well-directed, action-oriented, accountable person—multiple minds acting in concert. A team is vastly different from an organizational unit, task force, or project group. To function as one, all team members have to operate on an equal footing. Hierarchical relationships dissolve. Members must share a common understanding of group goals and strategies. Although members play different roles in pursuing goals, all work to hold each other equally accountable for performance and results (Katzenbach & Smith, 1993).

It ought to be obvious from this description that teams do not automatically emerge and become instantaneously effective—on sports fields or in more formal organizational contexts. Yet organizational leaders, for the most part, behave as if the basic ingredients of team-work are present among their staff almost through birthright. I have worked with countless groups, all dubbed "teams" by their super-visors, that lacked a common understanding of goals and had virtually no capacity for productive discussion in the service of task and no mutual agreements about individual assignments and reporting responsibilities.

Firm foundations must be laid before a team can successfully get on with its task. First, there must be basic ground rules for team interaction to which all members subscribe—do's and dont's defining behavior that are facilitative rather than obstructive. Members must also arrive at a shared understanding of the nature and dimensions of the task in front of them. They must explore differences in their individual perspectives and identify the common ground that binds them with regard to their assignment. Last, they need a unified approach to the way their task will be pursued and progress will be measured—exactly who will do what by when.

Talking and listening effectively in a group, consciously shaping the group task to fit individual capacities and vice versa, and explicitly assigning responsibilities for meeting common expectations are abili-ties not generally considered part of our genetic endowment. They are environmentally induced, specifically through good teaching.

The exercises in this section invite participants to build a solid foundation for teamwork. They contain a continuum of necessary ingredients, the absence of which will cause teams to founder.

- Discussion Functions and Concentric Conversations help group members hone their discussion skills, offering them practice at listening carefully to each other and developing common threads and themes.

- Working Norms and Marking Effective Teamwork assist groups in establishing and reinforcing guidelines that will govern their interactions over the course of work together.

- My Spot engenders an appreciation of individual perspectives and the need for all members to reach out in the direction of each other's thinking.

- Planning From the Ground Up exemplifies a progression from individual idea and perspective to group vision and strategy.

- Shaping the Future promotes the need for a common understanding of a task before plowing in and the desirability of mutual accountability for progress and results.

CONCENTRIC CONVERSATIONS

Purposes

Concentric Conversations draws all members of a group into intense one-on-one conversations on topics of consequence and encourages them to summarize, synthesize, and refine ideas that surface in these conversations. The exercise also offers individuals the opportunity to practice good listening skills and to mull over others' perspectives on problems. Done well, it helps a group come to terms with one of the most difficult aspects of teamwork, mutual accountability for performance.

Setup

No special equipment is needed for Concentric Conversations, only enough floor space for groups to stand and converse. An easel with newsprint sheets comes in handy for the debrief that follows the first part of the exercise.

In advance of the activity, the facilitator develops a set of questions that equates to the number of people in each circle (see the instructions below). If the total group is large, with several pairs of circles, the same number of questions will suffice. Each question is framed so as to build on the idea contained in the preceding question. Consider, for example, this set of questions, meant to guide a group charged with a special project:

1. What were your expectations about what you could achieve on this project when it was assigned to you?

2. What do you see as the central aims of the project?

3. Given these aims, can you speculate about the special capacities you yourself bring that will make the project a success?

4. Taking into account the capacities you and your last partner talked about, what strategy do you think the group ought to pursue on this project?

5. What constraints stand in the way of your completing the project?

6. How might you best circumvent or overcome the constraints you and your last partner discussed?

7. What measures ought you use to evaluate group progress on this project?

The list of potential questions is endless, as are the ways they can be sequenced. Facilitators should identify an overarching theme and a series of questions that supports it. Questions have to be open-ended yet cogent enough to compel multiple, intense head-to-head conversations. They also have to be succinct and clear, usually containing no more than one easy-to-remember idea. Taken together, the responses to the questions should provide coherent material that participants will find informative.

The activity and debrief together can take as little as a half hour, as much as an hour.

Instructions

The facilitator begins by asking all participants to stand. The facilitator then divides them into groups of 8 to 14. An even number is essential, even if attaining it requires the facilitator's participation. Each group of 8 to 14 forms two concentric circles in an open space on the floor, the outer circle of participants facing the center, the inner circle of participants facing the circumference. The result is that every person is facing one other person. For a group of 14, there should be 7 members in each circle; for a group of 8, there should be 4 in each circle. Illustration 4.1 shows the appropriate configuration of participants.

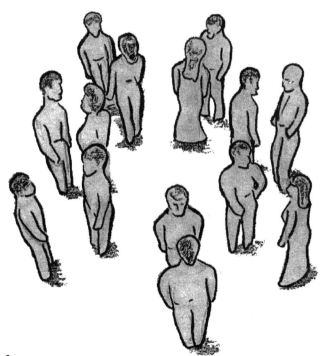

Illustration 4.1.

With all properly positioned, the facilitator poses the first question and asks participants to discuss it face-to-face for 5 minutes. All pairs are meant to discuss the same question. The facilitator reminds everyone that only 5 minutes are available, so "airtime" should be shared equally between the two discussants.

The succeeding order of moves is as follows. When time for the first conversation has expired, the facilitator asks those in the inner circle (or outer—it doesn't matter which) to rotate one person to the right. Everyone in the circles is now paired off with a different person. The facilitator then poses question two; vigorous discussion ensues; when time is up, the facilitator cuts off discussion and asks the outer or inner circle to rotate one person to the right; the facilitator poses the next question, and so on.

Following the stand and converse portion of the exercise, the facilitator asks the participants to cite the major points from their several conversations and summarizes them on the newsprint sheets. One way to do this is to array the sheets on the wall, each headed by one of the questions previously posed. The facilitator asks the entire group—there may have been more than one set of concentric circles—to think about recent conversations and point out some of the most intriguing points made by their partners, not by themselves. The facilitator records these points as they are recalled and synthesizes them as each sheet is filled. This process can take up to half an hour.

Success Markers

Concentric Conversations often yields a wealth of provocative material for future deliberations by a group. All of it is from the participants interacting with one another, not from the facilitator. If done well, the exercise can demonstrate the substantial benefits of collaborative inquiry.

A paramount consideration is the decibel level in the room as a measure of the intensity and focus in the conversations. Even if there is hesitancy at the beginning, that is, with the first pairs, there should be a cresting of participant enthusiasm as the activity unfolds.

One way to achieve a satisfactory result is to shut down conversations just as the decibel level is about to fall off. Another is to be rigorous in drawing out and synthesizing participants' points in the debrief that follows the face-to-face conversations. It is always satisfying to see the positive yield of collective effort.

Strategic Considerations

Concentric Conversations is an excellent introduction, or even inter-mediate review, for a group setting out on a task. It is less useful for a group that has reached a more advanced stage. The exercise is an efficient means of engaging all in a group, however large, in wrestling with major questions that define its task. A working group of 14, for example, will in the context of the activity have completed 49 short but intense conversations. Every person will have talked with seven different colleagues—all this in the space of about 40 minutes.

Following the summarization of points made in the multiple conversations between pairs, the facilitator conducts a separate debrief for the whole group on the effect of the activity.

Questions

- ✦ What was notable about the several conversations you had with your colleagues? What insights or surprises did they produce?

- ✦ What were your reactions to talking about issues in this fashion? Was it frustrating, fulfilling? In what ways?

- ✦ Looking at what is on the newsprint sheets, did the exercise generate compelling ideas in response to the questions asked? If so or not, what do you believe was the cause?

- ✦ What sorts of things did you learn from this exercise about solving problems? About generating and capturing good ideas for solving problems?

- ✦ How does your experience of this exercise advance your thinking about solving real problems in real organizations?

- ✦ The exercise is an artifact, a game. Nonetheless, are there applications from it that pertain to your work?

WORKING NORMS

Purposes

Working Norms is an exercise about establishing and maintaining operating rules in support of teamwork. The product of the exercise is a set of written working norms. These form a foundation for effective and efficient group discussions and more productive interactions in general among people who work together. If an organization has a published code of conduct, Working Norms will add substance to it. The intent is to produce something that is more than a set of general guidelines, something specific enough to affect daily practices.

Setup

The exercise requires only "post-it" notes and a wall or board to stick them on. Although the initial framing of working norms can be achieved in less than an hour, revising them, in the light of group experience, can—and should—consume several additional hours. The exercise can be done easily with groups of up to 30.

Instructions

The facilitator begins by engaging a group in an exhaustive discussion of the tasks and functions that make up its assignment. This must be done crisply, yet with ample specificity. To assist the group, the facilitator should carefully inventory beforehand the tasks and functions as he or she sees them. Many will be so obvious that they might easily be overlooked. Here is one such inventory:

- Considerable time spent as a whole group discussing goals and objectives

- At the same time, the group may split the task into more manageable pieces, with each member going off to inquire into certain areas, later reporting findings back to the whole group

- Sometimes there may be a need for smaller group work that will go on without much base touching with the group as a whole

- Each member may have to do some writing

- Together, the members of the group will have to compose a written team report for its supervisor, to be completed by a certain date

- After approval of the report, the group will have certain implementation tasks to perform

- It will also have to devise and apply certain evaluative measures
to determine progress as it proceeds with its task

The crux of the exercise is as follows: With these tasks and functions
in mind—including the ones the group has added—what operating
rules should group members agree to adhere to throughout their work
together—with each other, before getting too far down the road?

The facilitator asks each group member to come up with five or so
rules and write each one on a separate post-it note. The facilitator
reminds participants that rules should be as clear and specific as
possible. They will be used to guide behavior and therefore should be
phrased in behavioral terms. "Showing mutual respect for others'
points of view in discussions," for example, is not a particularly useful
rule. More helpful is "Members should positively acknowledge the
points made by others, build on them when possible, and express
disagreement with restraint, focusing at all times on the argument
made, not the attributes of the arguer."

When all participants have completed their post-its, they go to the
wall and paste them up. The facilitator then designates a group of about
five people to examine the entries posted on the wall and formulate an
initial framework that embraces all of them. The framework should
include no more than half-a-dozen categories. The facilitator then asks
succeeding groups of about five each to refine the framework their
predecessor group has produced—recast categories, eliminate duplica-
tive entries, highlight areas of disagreement among entries.

Now, with a draft framework in hand that all have had a part in
shaping, the whole group discusses it. Participants deliberate its appropriateness and its usefulness, and wrestle with areas of disagreement
and seek resolution of them. Eventually a rough consensus on a group
contract emerges. The role of the facilitator, among other things, is to
ensure that consensus is not arrived at by making its ingredients so
general as to be behaviorally neutral.

Success Markers

One key is specificity, and from my experience it is difficult to achieve.
Groups, however willing and primed, seemed compelled to recreate
the Bill of Rights rather delineate specific concerns that relate to their
work. Although the facilitator may incur resistance, he or she should

persist in having the group address matters that are likely to inhibit progress, stumbling blocks that will cause bickering and engender mutual dissatisfaction down the road. There is, for example, no more efficient drain on group enthusiasm than the feeling on the part of some that others are not pulling their weight. The group might need prompting to surface this concern and see that it is addressed.

Strategic Considerations

Timing is everything with this exercise. In almost all cases, it should be one of the very first exercises a project team does. At the same time, it may not be necessary to finalize working norms before proceeding with the initial phases of a project. The most desirable sequence is for a group to arrive at a first draft of working norms, then revise them in the wake of some preliminary interactions with each other.

Some readers, understanding the intent of this exercise, might wonder if it really is useful, particularly in well-established organizations or professional groups with solid canons of professional behavior. My experience is that the exercise is not only useful but absolutely essential. If a group bypasses the territory the exercise covers and just sets out on its task, it can find itself engulfed in misunderstanding and divisiveness that precludes high performance.

It is astonishing to me that group members who have worked with each other for years have no operating rules to govern their discussions with each other. In the same way that many people think good parenting skills automatically accrue with time, most denizens of organizations apparently regard team-working norms as givens that come with one's employment papers.

In contrast, it is a source of gratification when, 6 weeks after arduous negotiations on working norms, a group member interrupts discussion and calls attention to what he or she believes is a violation of the mutual contract. At this juncture, I am whispering to myself, as some of the participants might be as well, that the struggle at the beginning was well worth it. The group might be able to move forward rather than get bogged down in a debilitating procedural mire.

Questions

The main question that a facilitator should insinuate repeatedly into group discussions is the extent to which members feel the exercise has produced a tool of value, one that advances their common work. Certainly there will be concrete evidence of usefulness in the course of a group's work together. This can come in the form of someone "calling time" in the midst of a meeting and drawing the attention of others to the established norms. Or it can be expressed by a group's publishing its norms for colleagues to see, or making sure that they are posted for every group meeting.

DISCUSSION FUNCTIONS

Purposes

This exercise helps group members become more productive at conducting discussions. This means

- having their voices heard by their colleagues while at the same time listening more intently to what others are saying;

- building on points others make rather than diverting the flow of discussion to their own pet topic; and

- drawing out others' contributions rather than focusing solely on the merits of their own points of view.

Setup

The only props needed for the exercise are 3×5 cards of different colors. On the cards are letters that denote specific discussion functions. The ones that I regularly use are as follows:

- **B** = Build on the point made by the previous speaker

- **NT** = Introduce a new topic into the discussion

- **Q** = Ask a question of a previous speaker or the group

- **I** = Interrupt the flow of the discussion

Each function is also assigned a different color; for example, the I or interrupt card is red. All participants receive the same array of cards, at least two Bs and one each of the NT, Q, and I cards, for a total of five cards. Illustration 4.2 shows what each "player's hand" might look like.

Granted, participants in discussions fulfill other important functions beyond the four just identified. Synthesizing points made by previous speakers is one example—an S, if you will. Facilitators may choose to add additional function cards if they wish. Yet they should understand that the intent is not to present participants with a set of cards that covers all conceivable discussion functions. Rather, it is to spur participants to conceive of others as they experience the exercise.

Prior to conducting the exercise, the facilitator selects a topic for the group to discuss. The topic should be central to the work of the

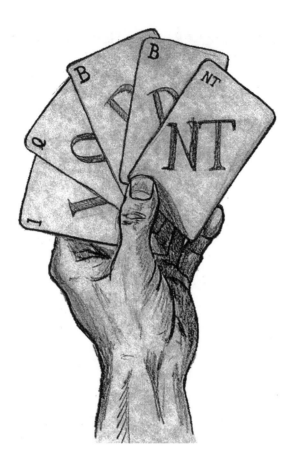

Illustration 4.2.

group, all the better if it is at the heart of its assignment, one that needs addressing before the group can move forward. The topic should be stated simply and clearly, usually in one sentence.

As a general rule, discussion groups should not exceed 12 members, so it may be necessary to form more than one group. The only spatial consideration is that all group members be able to see and hear each other. With more than one discussion in progress, each will need enough space to allow all members to listen carefully to each others' points. The exercise normally takes about an hour, activity and debrief together.

Instructions

After the groups settle into their discussion circles, the facilitator passes out identical sets of cards to each discussant. The facilitator states the topic he or she wants discussed and explains the constraints under which participants are to conduct the discussion. They must "play a card" before entering the discussion. When they have used that card, they must discard it. When a discussant no longer has cards to play, he or she can no longer participate in the discussion. Trading of cards among players is not allowed.

Success Markers

Discussions held under the conditions imposed by the exercise usually take a few minutes to gain intensity and rhythm. At the outset, there is considerable awkwardness that is hard for discussants to overcome. After about 20 minutes, the intensity tends to crest and then subside, thus signaling that it is time to end. At this point, some participants have exhausted their supply of cards and many have become weary of conversing under such artificial and constrained circumstances. That participants express frustration, or even evidence resistance to the rules of the game, should not cause concern. The facilitator should maintain a firm demeanor throughout, knowing that there will be much to talk about in the debrief.

Strategic Considerations

Discussion Functions can have the most beneficial effect on a group as its deliberations are getting underway. It is excellent preparation for the formal discussions that group members will have with each other over the course of their project. If successful, the exercise can aid in fostering good discussion citizenship, inclusive of guidelines understood and adhered to by all. The exercise provides good grist for both Working Norms and Marking Effective Teamwork.

Questions About What Happened

+ What was it like to have a discussion under these circumstances?

+ What coping strategies did you employ for dealing with the constraints imposed by the exercise?

+ Did you buck the constraints, or try to circumvent them? How so?

+ As you were engaged in the discussion, did you think of other functions that were not listed on the cards? What were they?

+ Did all of you use your full complement of cards? How many cards were left unused? Let's count the unused ones and look at which kind were used least.

+ Did some of you have more unused cards than others? If you used very few of your cards, or alternatively all of them, why was that?

Questions About Implications

+ What were the advantages of having a discussion in this way? What were the disadvantages?

+ Did the advantages outweigh the disadvantages, or vice versa?

+ What interpretation do you place on the fact that there were so many unused cards at the end of the discussion—or, if it was the case, so few unused cards at the end?

+ That some used all their cards and others used very few—does this matter? Does more even use of cards, that is, more uniform participation, have anything to do with whether discussions are successful?

+ What else did you learn from this exercise about effective discussions?

Questions About Applications

+ That you have important group work to do with each other is a given. That discussions with each other are integral to that work is a given. What can you distill from this exercise that will help improve the quality and productivity of your discussions?

+ Which specific measures regarding roles and levels of participation in discussions should you formally incorporate into the way you interact with each other in formal discussions?

+ In fact, which lessons are you willing to promise to bring into those interactions? Perhaps you should compose a draft code of discussion citizenship and make it part of your Working Norms.

PLANNING FROM THE GROUND UP

Purposes

This exercise assists a group in molding a durable consensus, a common point of view with a reasonable chance of holding up over time because all members have participated actively in shaping it. Its aim is what Peter Drucker (1974) refers to as an "effective decision," one that adheres rather than disappears. The exercise does this by assuring every member multiple opportunities to affect the thinking of fellow members along the path of deliberation.

Planning From the Ground Up is the antithesis of the appointed leader or a segment of a group imposing its will on the rest of the group. The exercise is particularly useful when a group has been showing signs of splintering on fundamental issues at the very point that agreement on those issues would substantially advance its work. The exercise is useful for large groups—20 or more—where consensus through other means is hard to come by.

Setup

No special props are needed for this exercise. The only requirement is enough working space to allow pairs of people to have separate discussions, then for foursomes to do the same, followed by groups of 8, 16, and so on. There should also be several newsprint sheets available to record points of agreement as well as points of disagreement, especially within each of the discussion groups that exceed four people. The exercise takes roughly 1 hour to complete.

Instructions

The facilitator begins by citing the topic, issue, or question he or she wants the group to discuss. It should be a matter on which the establishment of common ground among members is of critical importance to group progress. The more global and abstract the topic, the greater the likelihood of agreement among members; the more context-specific and concrete, the greater the likelihood of disagreement. The facilitator has to peg the question just right on this continuum to get positive results.

Proposing, for example, that a group of education and community leaders discusses implementable measures to promote closer working relationships between schools and community service agencies will produce a better result than asking it to focus on school-community bonds in general. Asking a group of business, government, and environmental leaders to wrestle with the fitness of a particular local development project will likely be more fruitful than a wide-ranging discussion of ecotourism.

After articulating the topic to be discussed, the facilitator asks the entire group to break into pairs, randomly. A possible variation on random pairing is to suggest that each person link up with another with whom there has been a demonstrable difference in view in past discussions. The pairs are asked to spend 5 to 10 minutes discussing the issue. The goal is to shape and record on newsprint sheets both the points on which discussants agree and those on which they do not agree.

The facilitator then asks each pair to join with another pair to form a foursome. These pairings are normally random, but can be intentional if desired. These newly formed groups of four recaps the results of the work in pairs, and then do as foursomes what they just did in pairs. The discussions may take up to 15 minutes.

After the foursomes have completed their discussions and recorded the results on newsprint sheets, the facilitator brings the entire group together and asks for reports from each of the foursomes. Based on what they produce, the facilitator highlights emerging areas of agreement and disagreement. He or she then doubles the size of the work groups to eight each, and gives them 20 minutes for preparation of a oral report for the entire group. Upon reconvening the whole group, the facilitator calls for group reports and again highlights emerging areas of agreement and disagreement.

The facilitator repeats this procedure, doubling the size of the work groups, reconvening them to gather the yield of their deliberations, and highlighting areas for further discussion, until the group is brought together again as one body. The facilitator concludes by conducting a final discussion with the group as a whole in which he or she asks group members to examine what they have done and to identify areas of common ground and areas of dispute.

Success Markers

Planning From the Ground Up presents many hazards to the advancement of group work, but it also offers great potential reward. Its success rests on three factors: the extent of good will within a group, the facilitator's ability to synthesize a host of viewpoints into a manageable short list, and a willingness on the part of all to accentuate areas of agreement without exaggerating them and to lay bare areas of disagreement without discounting their importance. Vibrant discussions at all levels and much nodding from participants in whole-group sessions are indicators that the exercise is having the desired effect.

Strategic Considerations

This is a difficult exercise to carry off well. I would not recommend attempting it in the early stages of group work. After discussion functions are perfected, working norms are in place, and group members have had enough time with each other to establish basic trust, Planning From the Ground Up may be in order. My experience with this exercise is that it can produce surprisingly positive results. Groups are startled to learn how much similarity of perspective there is within them, sometimes in areas they did not expect. They are also startled by how much diversity of perspective there is in areas they did not expect.

Questions

The debrief should be short because the most important yield from the exercise is the treatment of the issue itself. Key questions are ones regarding implications and applications. There is likely to be little dispute among participants about what occurred.

+ How does the sequence of short discussions you experienced in this exercise compare to less structured group processes? What effect did the discussion building blocks—pairs, foursomes, and so on—have on the group's attaining common ground? What effect did they have on the group's surfacing areas of disagreement? Were they helpful or not? In what ways?

+ If there were identifiable advantages to a building-block approach, how can you adapt it for use in your regular deliberations? More specifically, how can you be sure to draw out both confirming and disconfirming perspectives from all group members to be sure that the consensus you reach is a more effective decision, one that will stand up over time?

MY SPOT

Purposes

My Spot provides group members with an opportunity to increase their understanding of the perspectives of their colleagues. The activity calls for participants to find an amenable space, to take some time to reflect on issues and problems relevant to their group's task, and then to acquaint fellow participants with the thoughts and feelings their chosen space has inspired. The exercise substantiates the benefits of "management by walking around." Its lessons are about appreciating others' points of view—an essential ingredient of effective teamwork—and the salutary effects of even brief moments of individual reflection.

Setup

The only props needed are squares made of somewhat durable yet easily transportable material, one for each participant. Carpet squares with foot-long sides, or even shirt cardboard, will suffice. The exercise normally consumes about an hour, including a short interim debrief of less than 10 minutes and a longer one of about 15 minutes at the end of the exercise. It works well with groups that range in size from about 10 to 30.

Instructions

The facilitator begins by supplying each group member with a square, his or her "spot." After all participants have one in hand, the facilitator instructs them to find a spot somewhere in the room or in a defined area of the building—or, best of all, if conditions allow, in a bounded space outdoors. The spots should be far enough apart so that it would be difficult for participants to converse with each other during the activity. Quiet time alone is the aim even if another person is 20 feet away.

The facilitator asks all to remain on their spots for about 15 minutes. While there, they should reflect on a key issue related to their common task. The facilitator can either frame this issue for them or ask them to spend the time identifying an issue they believe the group should address. If the facilitator chooses to assign a topic, it should be ripe for individual reflection, one whose importance has been re-inforced by the group's recent experiences together. Writing materials come in handy for this, allowing participants to jot down notes regarding their reflections while on their spots. The final, yet essential, point the facilitator makes before participants disperse is that they should leave behind the object marking their spots, wherever placed, when they are called back to discuss the activity.

After the time allotted for individual reflection, the facilitator walks around and rounds up all participants, reminding them if necessary to leave their spots behind. When they reconvene, they form a discussion circle and the facilitator conducts a short debrief. The facilitator asks for comments on what it was like for participants to have their own spot, whether any participants care to note why they chose the spot they did, and whether anyone wishes to share ideas that occurred to them while on their spot. Although it will likely come up anyway, the facilitator also asks if this period of reflection, although brief, seemed like a small gift participants might want to award themselves on a regular basis.

Then, with a touch of fanfare, the facilitator says that there is a second part to the exercise. The entire group, with all members maintaining physical contact with each other, has to get everyone to everyone's spot, efficiently and effectively. Obviously this may be awkward with a group of 25, but so be it. The group is allowed to confer briefly to figure out how to do this. But, having decided on an approach to making their rounds and having begun to move as a unit, members can no longer talk with each other about tactics or progress. The only allowable conversation along the route is for group members at their will to describe why they chose the spot they did, as the group pauses to take note of it. All need not avail themselves of this opportunity, but everyone has to "get to everyone's spot." The facilitator accompanies the group as it proceeds. When it returns to its point of origin, having reached and acknowledged everyone's spot, a full debrief unfolds.

Success Markers and Strategic Considerations

Choosing the right time to do this exercise is key, both within the total time available for group work and within the frame of a given day. With regard to the former, My Spot is a respite from demanding and thought-provoking work that has been foundational, and also a means of collecting up the physical and intellectual energy for tougher challenges ahead. So the exercise is best lodged in the middle of things—after a group has been launched on its task, but before it gets too far down the road, that is, after considerable spade work but before intense synthesizing and forward-looking deliberation.

With regard to the latter, the exercise seems to work best at times of day when participants are ready for pause and reflection. Right after lunch is one of these times, as is midmorning, or more likely, mid-afternoon. At such junctures, participants are physiologically in need of a break from acute problem solving or active listening. The sitting, quiet reflection, and gentle movement of My Spot can provide welcome refreshment. I have found that it is even possible to substitute My Spot for a formal break, without incurring complaints from participants.

Beyond choosing the right time to do the exercise, the facilitator can foster success by maintaining a formal demeanor as he or she asks group members to join together and get everyone to everyone's spot. For some groups, this task can verge on being "touchy-feely," especially if they conclude that the only way to accomplish the task is to hold hands. Mild resistance in the form of nervous frivolity is one sure sign of this. Yet facilitator firmness is normally worth it, because the debrief will likely uncover interesting trade-offs regarding "getting everyone to everyone's spot" in real organizations.

The debrief should build on, perhaps even recapitulate, some of the main points made in the short group discussion following the individual reflection part of the activity.

Questions About What Happened

+ What strategy did you adopt for getting all the members of the group around to everyone's spot?

+ Were there difficulties you encountered in accomplishing the task? Any frustrations you experienced?

+ What were the advantages and disadvantages of the approach you chose?

+ Describe the communication that took place between the person whose spot was being highlighted and the rest of the group.

+ How did you construe the essential task of this exercise as you were engaging in its activities? How did you construe its essential task in the wake of having done the activities? Were these the same, similar, or different?

Questions About Implications

+ How important is it to get everyone to everyone's spot? Is this important in organizations? Why or why not?

+ Is it important to you that others understand why you chose the spot you did? Why or why not? Is there an organizational parallel here?

+ Talk about the trade-offs you made as a group between efficiency and effectiveness in getting everyone around to everyone's spot. If, for example, "getting the silly thing over with as quickly as possible" characterizes your mode, what does this say about your willingness to begin tasks in the context of shared understanding of purpose?

+ What did you learn about other people's inclinations and perspectives?

+ What did you learn about the extent to which this group honors others' inclinations?

Questions About Applications

+ How important is the provision of time for individual and group reflection to the work of this group? If it is important, what do you intend to do to find a fit place for it?

✦ Based on what you have discussed in this debrief, would you have any suggested amendments to the working norms this group developed earlier?

✦ "Getting everyone to everyone's spot" could be viewed as step one on a path that leads to consensus decision making. How far down this path do you want to go? Which aspects of this mode of doing things do you want to insert into your work with each other?

✦ If you viewed the essential task of this exercise differently after having done it, what does this mean for your planning and goal setting, functions that are supposed to dictate essential tasks before they take place?

SHAPING THE FUTURE

Purposes

Whenever people embark on a new assignment together, they are unsighted in important respects. They do not know what the future will bring. The demands imposed by their task are unknown to them. If they have not worked together as a group, they do not know what their interactions will be like. Shaping the Future offers participants the opportunity to work together at a task without the benefit of sight. It invites them to achieve a greater common understanding of a task and to determine responsibilities for evaluating progress in accomplishing it. Because the exercise presents problems of both goal definition and mutual accountability for evaluation, it is an excellent team building experience.

Setup

The exercise normally consumes about an hour, including a full half hour for debriefing. It works best with groups of between 15 and 25. Props include blindfolds for the participants, a 40- to 50-foot length of rope, and a deck of playing cards.

Instructions

The facilitator begins by asking participants to stand in a loose circle and don blindfolds. Rolled bandannas normally suffice. As people are putting on their blindfolds, the facilitator reassures them that the exercise is perfectly safe and that he or she will remain sighted at all times and be present throughout. Such assurances are unnecessary for most, but those for whom temporary blindness engenders slight fear may need to have them.

When all are unsighted, the facilitator walks around the inside of the circle placing the rope into the outstretched hands of each participant. If possible, the facilitator provides for some slack in the rope at different points and makes sure that the two participants closest to the rope ends are not aware that they are holding the ends (see Illustration 4.3).

After the rope is distributed, the facilitator tells the participants that their task as a group is to form a perfect square. The facilitator says that they may talk with each other to complete the task. In conclusion, the facilitator asks if there are any questions, being sure to

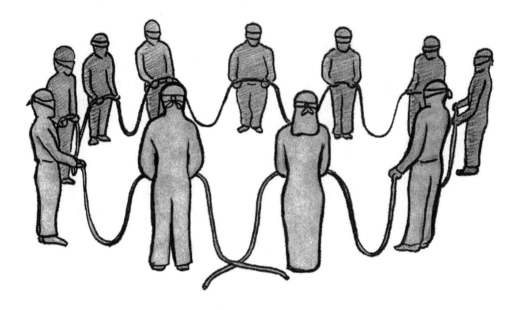

Illustration 4.3.

answer only those that do not deprive participants of the opportunity to wrestle with the ambiguities the directions offer. "To form a perfect square" can be interpreted in a number of ways.

An enriching variation on the above format is to insert playing cards into the rolled bandannas of the participants, one, two, three, four, or five cards, distributed randomly. As the facilitator places cards in each participant's blindfold, he or she says out loud how many cards there are. With these additional props in place, the facilitator amends the instructions to say that for the first 10 minutes of the group's deliberations, participants are allowed to talk freely with each other. After that time, they may offer only as many contributions to the conversation as they have cards available. Following each contribution, they must discard. When participants have expended their supply of cards, they may no longer talk.

Success Markers

Typically, the activity unfolds as follows. The problem solving begins with a cacophony of suggestions, all shouted out at once. Yet, although few relate to the nature of the task, almost all relate to how to do it; that is, the making of a perfect square with the rope. One person sheepishly puts forth the idea that the group should make a perfect square with the people, not the rope. But that idea is trampled in a stampede toward the "right" definition. Then another person suggests selecting only four people from the whole group to make a square with the rope. That idea is dismissed too in favor of using all the bodies as well as the rope. After much haggling and debate about procedures and approaches, a rough square of rope takes shape.

Then discussion turns to determining "Are we done?" and "Can we remove our blindfolds?" Someone from the group asks where the facilitator is and suggests, or demands, that he or she make those decisions. If playing cards are used, a gap emerges between vocal and nonvocal participants in the initial problem solving phase and carries through to the restricted discussion phase as well. Chaotic interchange, precipitous moves in response to ill-conceived ideas, dissonance about strategy and completion of task—these and variations of them all contribute to a rich debrief.

Strategic Considerations

The decision to take away people's sight should be made conservatively and only after a facilitator becomes familiar with participants' risk-taking threshold. Because the issues the exercise raises—group goal determination and mutual responsibility for evaluation of results—are central to team formation, fitting the exercise into the early stages of group work makes sense. At the same time, because the activity engenders fear in some, doing it first does not make sense.

Groups generally derive a significant sense of collective accomplishment from this exercise. This is abetted perhaps by the sheer relief of getting the blindfolds off. It is therefore wise to do the exercise when a "high" might offset apprehension about future challenges and the group's ability to step up to them.

Questions About What Happened

+ What was it like to be unsighted?

+ How did you compensate for your loss of sight?

+ What did you as a group do to solve the problem you were asked to? Who did what? For example, who made oral suggestions or took an initiating role by making physical moves? Which suggestions were accepted by the group as the way to go? Which ones were dismissed? (As an aside, getting a group to create a detailed account of what happened may not be easy, but it is essential. A thorough and comprehensive set of observations supports common understanding and effective group action.)

+ What was the task of this exercise in your view, and how did the group arrive at that definition of task? Were there any reservations voiced about the task as defined and carried out?

+ What was your interpretation of the word "perfect"?

+ Describe the sequence of events that led to your removing your blindfolds. As you were getting close to thinking you were finished, who said what? Who did what?

+ What occurred as a result of your having to use playing cards to make your voice heard in the problem solving? Did the number of cards you had available make a difference in terms of what you said and how many times you talked? How did the unequal distribution of cards affect the behavior of those who had been more vocal in the open discussion period? How about those who had been less vocal?

Questions About Implications

+ In retrospect, would you do anything differently to determine what the group task really entailed? Would you have shaped your initial discussions differently?

+ How did the group sort through the various suggestions that were made? How did some become "gospel" and others get passed over? How, in effect, would you describe your decision-making process? What did you learn from all this about the dynamics of group decision making?

+ What difference does it make if some people are granted more voice, that is, more cards, than others in this group?

+ Comment on the discussion you had during the activity regarding who was responsible for determining when the task was successfully accomplished and how that should be done. What was the balance between the facilitator's responsibility and your own for assessing quality and sufficiency?

Questions About Applications

+ What can you carry from this exercise into your real group work, which in itself requires a common framing of task at the outset with as much buy-in from all members as possible? How are you going to go about that—the same way you did it in this exercise, or differently?

+ What about the issue of distributing the power of voice? Are there direct applications to your work together? What would you do to see that as many voices as possible get heard?

+ How do you want to distribute responsibility within the group for assessing progress and results? What relationship do you want to craft between you and your group leader for this essential function? In very practical terms, if you want to distribute responsibility widely, what steps will you take to be sure that each group member does this, contributes to determining when you have made "a perfect square" and can move on to the next challenge?

MARKING EFFECTIVE TEAMWORK

Purposes

The purpose of this exercise is to create a code of acceptable behavior in support of effective teamwork. Teams can use this code as a continuing source of guidance as work on their task proceeds. Marking Effective Teamwork builds on Working Norms and Discussion Functions. The latter two are preliminary, offering a group initial guidance as it sets out on its task, ensuring that it does not have to double back and discuss matters that should have been ironed out at the beginning. Marking Effective Teamwork prompts a group to generate a refined product, one that contains definite behavioral cues that help group members govern themselves over the full term of their work together.

Setup

The sole prop is a draft code of team citizenship. The draft is normally developed after the group has completed enough of its work that members recognize its ingredients as relevant to their prior interactions. Although portions of the draft can come from group members as well as the facilitator, the latter should take responsibility for pulling it together. The exercise normally takes an hour or more to complete.

The draft code in Chart 4.1 emerged from my work with one organization. It may be a useful starting point for others to develop their own. The directive in it apply to all group members.

Instructions

The facilitator presents the draft to the team and asks members to consider its contents in detail. The facilitator calls for specific references to recent team behavior and seeks confirmation from the team regarding inclusion or exclusion of each point.

Depending on the numbers of participants, it may make sense to divide a group into smaller units to consider a draft like the one in Chart 4.1. The facilitator can then reconvene the whole group to synthesize suggestions for additions, deletions, and amendments. Differences in points of view within and between small groups are themselves good material for discussion in the larger group.

Success Markers and Strategic Considerations

Signs of group readiness to engage with a draft code ought to be apparent: Members discuss its substance with ease; they openly make reference to recent interactions that attest to the validity of certain points in the draft; and they eagerly confirm inclusion or exclusion of particular elements.

The exercise normally takes an hour or slightly more. If that time frame is exceeded or the discussion starts to feel awkward, a group may be experiencing divisions that will not be healed through this exercise, and in fact could be exacerbated by it. If this is the case, the facilitator should try other means of surfacing and resolving differences. See the exercises relating to managing conflict in the succeeding section, particularly Voices.

Questions for Marking Effective Teamwork

One important line of questioning relates to the code's applicability to the operation of the organization as a whole.

+ Are some parts applicable and others not?

+ Is the code useful only for the team's work, or does the process and product represented have broader value within the organization?

+ What do the answers to these questions say about working relationships in the wider organization?

CHART 4.1. A Draft Code of Team Citizenship

- Clarify in your head the task the group is about to undertake, contribute to clarifying it, cajole fellow members for clarification, and, if necessary, demand clarification.

- Fix your thoughts on the outcomes of team efforts and, in your own head, assess progress—"This is what we said we were going to do by the end of the month—how are we doing, have we done it, how well have we done it?"

- If a team member or someone outside the team says, "You can't do that because this rule or guideline or this individual or group won't allow it," question this assertion with all the diplomacy you can muster and gain verification that the barrier really exists. The barrier may be more bluster than bar.

- Listen to and analyze pronouns used by others in-group discussions. I is often honest and forthright, but too much I and not enough we can put fellow team members off and result in distorted relationships that will hamper progress. Be a bit wary of too much you; it could mean a shifting of responsibility away from where it belongs, that is, placing blame, which is the bane of effective teamwork. The we of "We are all in this together" is usually helpful, unless it involves a subtle unwillingness to accept individual responsibility. But the we that is royal, that is, prideful and exclusive, usually results in walls being built where they are not needed. Finally, the they that is ominous and threatening, the enemy without, may be a cover for internal shortcomings. If you are uncomfortable about a we or they, ask and get an answer to who the we or they is.

- Actively seek other team members' point of view in all discussions, especially those that result in decisions; do not focus solely on your own. Say to a fellow member, "What do you think about this proposed direction? You have been doing some important work on a key aspect of it, so it would be useful to hear what you think."

- Demonstrate that you are listening carefully to what someone else has said by occasionally "playing it back" to them and to the rest of the group.

- Build on comments and contentions made by others—"I'd like to add to what she just said by suggesting . . ." and when you do this, be sure that what you say really relates to the point just made, that it isn't a separate point cloaked as a complementary one.

- Feel free to throw kudos of all kinds into the open forum of group discussion. For example, offer compliments for colleagues' exhibitions of discussion citizenship such as those noted above. Relay negative comments to colleagues in private, off to the side of group discussions. Don't pollute team waters.

- When pressed by others in a group discussion, resort to the authority of knowledge—to homework done and perspective gained. Do not resort to the authority of position, age, or seniority, either yours or someone else's.

- When disagreeing with a teammate, stick to the issue; stay away from character, do not characterize another's comments or behavior.

Exercises on Managing Conflict

Introduction

Conflict, it is said, is endemic to organizational functioning. Learning how to "manage" it is one of the things expected of those who aspire to leadership in organizations. Managing conflict does not mean, however, hoping it will go away, or worse yet, denying its existence. Nor does it mean reconciling oneself to life in Harry Truman's kitchen, that is, "taking the heat or getting out." A middle course, somewhere between these two, is the most sensible. It is one that encourages acceptance of conflict as inevitable, yet at the same time assists people in developing capacities to harvest the benefits of conflict, rather than perpetually reaping its liabilities.

When it comes to effective management of conflict, the current literature on leadership is not particularly helpful. It brims with unrealistic exhortations about collaboration and communication, community building, and teamwork (Kaagan, 1997). Rarely does it probe the roots, realities, and effects of conflict. Most organizational denizens are left to their own devices, struggling toward a mode of dealing with conflict that suits and serves them but never being quite sure if they are hitting the mark.

The principal focus of the exercises that follow is the roots of conflict. Here are some of those roots, disentangled from each other, and particular exercises that will assist emerging leaders in understanding and coming to terms with them:

- Gross miscommunication between individuals and groups: Witch and Watch

- False assumptions about others' intentions: Ritual Conflict

- People's natural inclination to compete rather cooperate, even when it clearly detracts from high performance: Tug of War and Bureaucracy

- The different values that different individuals and groups hold dear: Voices and Ritual Conflict

- People's inclinations to be contrary under the pressure of deadlines: Evacuation Drill

- Constraints imposed by the highly structured relationships that develop in hierarchical organizations: Bureaucracy

- The conflicting expectations of leaders as against followers: Leaders' Walk.

Taken together, the exercises provide a rich laboratory in which participants can experience conflict and discuss how to take advantage of it rather than the other way around. The exercises offer controlled conditions and low stakes. These facilitate participants' gaining increased understanding about the dynamics of conflict, opening more to its potential for advancing rather detracting from a cause, and beginning to shape their own unique approach to capitalizing on it. Such outcomes cannot be achieved by reading about conflict management, listening to experts talk about it, or deliberating with coworkers about how conflict plays out in their work contexts.

WITCH AND WATCH

Purposes

This exercise introduces participants to difficulties associated with communication in organizations, particularly ones with hierarchical structures. It highlights the inevitable conflicts that arise as cross-currents of information sweep through an organization. For staff who pursue their assignments assuming that good communication develops in the absence of carefully worked out procedures to fit varying circumstances, the exercise is a powerful object lesson.

Setup

The exercise usually takes less than an hour. It is best done with groups of about 15 to 30. The main props are two objects of different color or character that can be passed easily from one participant's hands to another participant's hands. Illustration 5.1 shows the basic configuration.

Illustration 5.1.

Instructions

To get underway, the facilitator asks participants to stand and form a circle. The facilitator calls their attention to two objects he or she is holding, one in each hand—for example, a blue magic marker and a red magic marker. Any easily distinguishable objects will suffice. The participator tells them that the blue marker is a "witch" and the red one a "watch," and states that the challenge as a group is to pass the objects around the circle, from one person to another, one object in one direction, the other in the opposite direction, until they return to their point of origin, that is, the facilitator.

The facilitator also notes that the participants must do this according to certain rules. Specifically, the facilitator is the sole authoritative source of information about what the objects in fact are, and his or her "blessing" regarding their identity has to be obtained in each instance before they can be passed on to the next person around the circle. The facilitator then demonstrates for the group what he or she means by these rules. The facilitator turns to the person to the right, holding the red marker in his or her hand, and says to that person, "This is a witch." The facilitator prods the potential recipient to say, "A what?" When she does, the facilitator responds matter-of-factly with, "A witch," and passes it to her.

At the urging of the facilitator, the person to the right then turns to the person to her right and repeats the interchange she just had with the facilitator. She says, "This is a witch." The person to her right says, "A what?" She is on the verge of saying, "A witch," but recalls (or, more likely, is reminded by the facilitator) that only the facilitator holds the essential information regarding identity that will allow a person in the circle to pass the object on to the next person. So when the person to the right of the facilitator is asked by the person to her right, "A what?" she must turn back to the facilitator and ask, "A what?" as well. The facilitator, in response, reiterates, "It's a witch." Armed with this vital information, the person to the facilitator's right can now convey both the information and the object to the person to her right.

The facilitator immediately initiates the same process to his or her left using the blue marker as a watch. Remember, even the sixth person down the line must secure the object's correct identity from the facilitator, by a series of five, passed-on queries, one after the other down the line, before being able to convey the object to the seventh person. Slowly and awkwardly, the two markers move from person to person, one to the left of the facilitator, the other to the right, according to the rules outlined and demonstrated above.

Success Markers

As the activity unfolds, the facilitator remains busy and attentive, answering the "A what?" from both left and right. The constituents, of course, struggle with the cumbersome procedure the facilitator has mandated. Laughter inevitably erupts as the silliness of it all sinks in. The eyes of participants eventually turn toward the part of the circle farthest from the facilitator, where the objects are about to cross. When they finally do, chaos reigns and a cacophony of laughter drowns out the crossfire of "A witch," "A what?" and "A watch."

The group, usually without any organized conferring, somehow regains its composure. By hook or crook, and with the help of one or more clear-headed participants, the group manages to pass the objects around the circle and return them to the hands of the facilitator. With sighs of relief, lingering laughter, and considerable banter, the debrief begins.

Strategic Considerations

Witch and Watch is an excellent opener. In fact, it works best with a group just beginning a project, not one that has established working norms and in which members know a great deal about each others' strengths and weaknesses. Because the exercise is fun, usually promoting much merriment, it takes the edge off apprehensions that group members might be carrying into an experience and allows them to lighten up, while at the same time posing critical issues about organizational functioning.

Questions About What Happened

+ What was the task you were assigned? Restate it.

+ What did you do as a group to overcome the challenge put in front of you? What, for instance, did you do immediately after you were given the assignment? Did you confer with each other about how you were going to proceed?

+ What happened when the two objects crossed? What did you do as it became apparent to several of you that there was going to be a problem at the point where they crossed?

+ As individuals, what did you do to address the obvious challenges, especially those of you who were caught at the crossroads of the information flow?

+ Did you develop some sort of system to deal with the procedural constraints placed on you? If so, how did you arrive at that particular system?

Questions About Implications

+ If you as a group made a decision not to confer with each other about the task at hand, why so? What do you make of this?

+ If you let chaos erupt, even when you saw it coming, why was that? Even after chaos broke out, your decision as a group was to muddle through without discussing the development of some sort of system to overcome the difficulties facing you. Why?

+ As a group you had a relatively simple task, to pass two symbolic objects from person to person around a circle. That you needed the "boss's" permission each time you wanted to make a move made the whole process very difficult. Let's discuss whether anything like this occurs in organizations with which you are familiar and whether you have experienced similar difficulties as result.

Questions About Applications

+ If the circumstances of the exercise fit your organization's—you have to go back to the boss to gain approval before taking even modest steps forward—what should be done about this?

✦ If you saw a communications debacle about to unfold in your organization, would you attempt to head it off? Do you have systems in your organization to deal with situations like this? Should you? What would such systems look like?

✦ The conflict that erupted in this exercise promised too many good laughs to want to head it off. Yet there is an important lesson here about conflicts that people regularly experience in organizations, conflicts both inside oneself and between oneself and others. How can you apply these lessons to your organization where the stakes—and the emotions—run much higher, and the outcomes are more consequential for both the organization and individuals who work in it?

BUREAUCRACY

Purposes

This exercise demands that participants maneuver around each other in extremely tight quarters. Significant problems of communication, perspective, and role differentiation arise and must be overcome. The exercise simulates well the difficulties of group problem solving in a highly structured organizations. When two groups do the exercise side by side in the same space at the same time, competition between the groups tends to drive out cooperation, even though cooperation has some obvious benefits.

Setup

The only equipment needed for the activity is masking tape or other appropriate material to mark spots on the floor. Enough open floor space to accommodate two parallel columns of between 10 and 14 participants, standing about 18 inches apart, is also a necessity. Diagram 5.1 depicts the layout as it would appear from above.

Although squares would be ideal to identify where participants should stand, single hash marks will do. About an hour should be set aside for the activity and debrief afterward.

Instructions

The facilitator introduces the activity with only a few sentences, suggesting that it is an opportunity for group problem solving and it offers special insight into the problems inherent in hierarchical organizations. The facilitator asks participants to proceed to the grid of squares or hash marks set up on the floor and for each participant to stand on a square, leaving vacant the square that has an X on it. Once all participants have taken up their positions, the facilitator asks them to face in the direction of the square with an X on it, that is, toward the middle of the column in which they are standing. If there are two groups, this means that in each column there will be two subgroups, with people lined up one behind the other facing the center point of the column. Illustration 5.2 shows this configuration.

The challenge, notes the facilitator, is for the members of the two subgroups to exchange places with each other. In the case of columns with an east-west orientation, those facing west need to wind up in the positions of those facing east. In the process of trying to accomplish

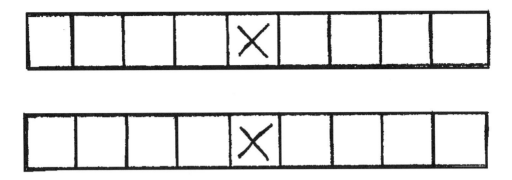

Diagram 5.1.

Illustration 5.2.

this exchange, however, members of the subgroups must observe certain rules, as follows:

- The only possible movement of participants is to a vacant square; in other words, participants facing each other may go around each other, but only if they use the vacant square to accomplish this maneuver.

- Participants facing in the same direction may not go around each other, regardless of the availability of a vacant square to do so.

- Participants may only move forward, that is, in the direction they are facing; in no instance can they move backward.

- A participant making a move can only go around one opposite-facing person at a time.

- Only one participant can be standing on a square at a time.

- Although participants can talk with each other freely to solve their common problem, they may not at any time stray from their assigned positions; there are only two exceptions to this rule—first, trial, error, and reset is allowed, and second, participants at the end of a column may rotate to the front at the will of the subgroup.

- Roughly half an hour is assigned the activity, although the facilitator may allow more time if the group is close to solving the problem.

- Participants are not to use paper and pencil, pennies, or other objects to simulate the problem; the only objects available to them are their bodies and minds.

As participants grope for a solution, the facilitator stands back and observes behavior, such as the relative levels of engagement of different participants, the extent of interaction between participants in the two separate columns if any, the nature of the brainstorming used to solve the problem, and the role of the group versus the individual in problem solving.

Success Markers

That some participants become disengaged from the activity or even overtly frustrated with lack of progress is not cause for concern. On the contrary, such reactions offer much to discuss in the debrief, for example, what it feels like to be out of the loop on a matter that affects you. In this exercise, the facilitator has to stick to his or her guns regarding the rules, not only those that distinguish legal from illegal moves but also those that apply to total group behavior, particularly the mandate that everyone remain in place on the grid throughout the activity. The learning from the exercise depends on tight compliance with the rules.

Strategic Considerations

Bureaucracy is best done after a group has engaged in team building and has met some success in working collaboratively on its main task. Because the activity is structured to allow only a few to be at the center of decision making, many participants feel extraneous to the problem solving at hand and unclear about how to help their colleagues. It is important, therefore, for a group to establish beforehand a solid foundation of positive working relationships. For some, the exercises can be quite sobering about the true extent of collaboration and teamwork in their organization. It makes sense that it be situated in the middle of a set of interventions, not at the start or at the end.

Questions About What Happened

- ✦ What was it like for you as participant to be solving this problem while caught in the middle of it?

- ✦ Since you could not move out of your position on the grid and could not create a simulation of the problem, how did you get the perspective necessary to solve the problem?

- ✦ I noticed some participants who were pretty disengaged, even perhaps slightly disgruntled; what was going on here?

- ✦ Describe the content and quality of communication within a given subgroup between those at the front of the line and those at the back.

- ✦ How did you in fact solve the problem, what did you do to solve it? Who played key roles in solving the problem, and what exactly did they do?

- ✦ What sort of interaction was there between the two groups lined up side by side and charged with solving the same problem?

Questions About Implications

- ✦ What were the difficulties involved in communicating effectively within the context of the constraints imposed by the activity? Within your subgroup, what was the character and quality of communication? What about between the two subgroups facing each other within each group?

- ✦ If there was not effective communication between the two groups working side by side, why was this? There was no bar to the two groups' communicating with each other, was there?

- ✦ If you worked in an organization where information flowed linearly from "front office" to "back office," what steps could you take to foster better communication?

- ✦ If you were in a situation where two separate groups had been assigned the same task, what steps could you take to foster better communication?

- ✦ If you agree that it would have been helpful to each group to engage the insights of other, what prevented you from doing this?

What does this say about how we solve problems in organizations? Is what happened in this activity reflective of what goes on in hierarchical organizations, or does it happen in all, regardless of how they are structured?

✦ What understanding does this exercise offer regarding the management of conflict in organizations, for example, the simmering conflict that arises out of being at the front of the line versus the back or being assigned to one of two work groups charged with solving the same problem?

Questions About Applications

✦ What can you do within your organization or your unit to address the quandaries this exercise poses—achieving effective communication in the midst of tight constraints, acquiring enough outside perspective to solve problems, overcoming the natural tendencies of people to compete rather than cooperate even when the latter has obvious benefits? Which of these would you tackle first and what specific steps do you recommend?

✦ In the context of projects you are working on, identify leadership moves you might make to counter the ill effects of hierarchical forms of communication, to gain adequate outside perspective, and to overcome the competitive ethic when it hampers progress.

EVACUATION DRILL

Purposes

Evacuation Drill is about allocating scarce resources in the midst of exigency. If a sense of urgency is created, participants can learn much about

- the dynamics of internal and interpersonal conflict;

- the advantages and disadvantages of collaboration under emergency conditions;

- the inevitable strain between meeting short-term needs and longer-term objectives; and

- the ever-present challenges of dealing with unfamiliar territory and uncertainty about the future.

Setup

The exercise requires careful site selection, thorough preparation, and appropriate props. To illustrate the importance of these requirements, let me relate the most intense version of the exercise I experienced as a participant. It took place on a small sailing craft anchored off an island in the Atlantic Ocean. The facilitator gathered our crew of 12 together at the end of a long day of sailing and said that we had one more exercise to do, called Evacuation Drill. He then said quite matter-of-factly that we had 10 minutes to evacuate the boat because it was going down. Other than what we had on our person at the moment, each of us could take one item from the boat for our stay on the island, which he speculated would last at least 1 night. We quickly conferred, collected our limited food and gear, and disembarked.

Although not offering as much drama as the situation just described, a private home could afford just as much challenge. Here the instructions might be for each participant to take one item from the house for a stay of indeterminate duration in a place of significant deprivation. One could also envision the exercise taking place in a public building where the drill would be to salvage a sense of the building's history from the ravages of an impending natural disaster. In sum, the facilitator has to take advantage of available sites that have the potential for meeting the objectives he or she has in mind.

Once the site is determined, it is necessary to ensure that it contains an array of objects from which participants must choose the few they will take with them. Fortunately, most American homes provide plenty to choose from, especially if one is about to depart immediately for a destination that boasts markedly fewer material advantages.

The activity, including the hurried discussion and ensuing evacuation, takes only about 20 minutes. The debrief can take up to an hour depending on how applicable the dynamics of the exercise are to the organizational challenges the group is confronting.

Instructions

The facilitator, having identified a site and ensured the availability of appropriate contents, tells the participants that a disaster looms, one that will require their ready removal from the premises. The facilitator explains that they have a set time, 15 minutes at most, to discuss which items to take with them—the equivalent of one object per person—be it for personal survival, historic preservation, or some other articulated purpose.

Success Markers

In explaining this activity to participants, the facilitator should in all instances adopt a serious demeanor and convey a clear sense of urgency. Participants should feel that they have no alternative but to confer quickly and make consequential choices, some of which will undoubtedly be wrong upon reflection. It is also important to make the total of items taken to be one item per person, setting up the tension between individual preference and group need.

Strategic Considerations

Because the exercise is about making tough choices within a tight time frame, it should come on the heels of a group's having experienced the benefits of teamwork. If done when a group is just getting down to work, the learning may be more ephemeral than enduring. The exercise can be quite engaging for a group that has worked together, had some initial success, but is now about to enter into uncharted territory, full of unprecedented conditions and a great deal of uncertainty.

Questions About What Happened

+ What objects did you decide to take? Let's look at them arranged on the floor, or on the table.

+ Put them into a rough order of priority—perhaps putting first the ones on which there was quick agreement.

+ What priorities dictated your choices? Were some of the criteria that affected your decision making not apparent at the time you were doing the activity, but are now?

+ What sorts of things did you talk about with each other to reach your decisions? Replay for me how your rapid-paced group deliberations unfolded.

+ In the midst of your discussions, were there things you as individual were thinking that you did not express to the group?

+ Describe the differences, if any, between the two thought processes, open group deliberation versus what was going on in your head.

Questions About Implications

+ You made some choices together about what to take with you into an uncertain future. Examining the sum total of your choices right now, would you reaffirm all of them?

+ Alternatively, would you be making different choices now? Are other more important criteria surfacing for you now after some time for reconsideration?

+ Can a group reach consensus about fit criteria, even in a very short time? How important is it that you agree on one or two key criteria, even if you only have 10 minutes to do so? What does this exercise tell you about the dynamics of and the requisites for effective collaboration?

+ What were the effects of your being forced to deal quickly with trade-offs between group and individual needs and goals? What did you learn about the relationship between what you wanted and what the group wanted?

+ Being pulled between objects that have enormous personal appeal versus objects that have clear utility for group welfare—this is not easy. How were these conflicts manifested and resolved? What are the implications of this for organizational functioning?

+ How do we fit together the preferences of individuals and the needs of organizations? Is it axiomatic that the former just give way to the latter? Should there be a compromise position, and how would you effect it?

Questions About Applications

+ Based on your performance in this exercise, how well equipped do you think you are to deal with the challenges that lie ahead in your project—as individuals and as a team?

+ Can you manage the inevitable conflicts between individual preferences and group needs that will arise? If not, what should you do to shore up that capacity? Are there, for example, resources you do not now have that you think you will need in the next phase of your work?

+ Can you cite a few decision rules that will likely affect your performance in this next phase of work? Write them down now and see how useful they are to you a month hence.

+ Evacuation Drill captures a piece of the perpetual drama of holding on to some things needed for the future while disposing of others that are not as necessary. How does this metaphor apply to your present circumstances? Are there things you want to carry with you no matter what, and things you would just as soon leave behind?

VOICES

Purposes

This exercise fosters a deeper understanding of the diversity of opinion that exists within a group on a controversial issue of consequence to its performance. The exercise can also help a group mold greater consensus on a tough issue before it. The success of the exercise depends on good facilitation skills—first, encapsulating a key issue in one well-phrased declarative sentence; and second, synthesizing multiple points of view into four or five clearly stated contentions. These contentions lay the ground for the refinement of individual perspectives and the identification of commonly held points of view.

Setup

There are minimal equipment and space needs for this exercise. Newsprint sheets and an easel are required, and enough floor space for participants to form a loose circle. The exercise works best with groups of between 15 and 20. It can take about an hour or more. If multiple groups do the exercise in the same space and time slot, additional time should be allotted at the end for a plenary discussion.

Instructions

The facilitator begins by asking participants to stand and form a circle, of which the facilitator is a part. With a few sentences, the facilitator recaps the topic at hand, asks for the active involvement of all, and asserts that what is learned in the exercise will be helpful in advancing the group's work. The facilitator then puts forth a one-sentence assertion about the topic and asks group members to formulate reactions to it.

A few years ago, for example, I was working with a group of business leaders, environmental activists, and government officials. Their aim was to support tourism that would be both economically and environmentally sound—a tall order in any case, but especially so for a group with such disparate points of view. One of the issues they had to address was land use planning. The statement I laid out before them in Voices was "Effective land use planning will require a significant shift away from private property rights as presently constituted." I knew that there was great diversity of opinion in the group on who should make land use decisions and how they should be made. I also knew the group had to achieve some common ground on these matters before it could proceed.

Having articulated a one-sentence contention, the facilitator uncovers a newsprint sheet on which the statement is written in large print, and then asks group members to think about their positions with respect to it. After a pause, the facilitator opens the floor and asks members to articulate their positions on the assertion just offered. The facilitator prods them by saying he or she is not just looking for a yes or no, but elaborated position taking—affirmative, negative, or a mix.

After four or five distinct positions on the assertion have surfaced—it may take 10 or more people talking before there are that many distinct positions—the facilitator intercedes. The facilitator carefully identifies the bellwether position takers by name and recites their positions as he or she understands them. He or she then asks all other participants in the group to walk to the place of the position taker whose "voice" best represents their own point of view, and cluster in a small circle around him or her.

The facilitator should carefully observe group members' "voting with their feet" to see if there are a few who are undecided about where to go. These people may have a separate and distinct point of view that they were hesitant to voice to the group. The facilitator may want to elicit their positions later.

When all arrive at their destination, these newly formed smaller groups discuss the position taken, and in the space of a few minutes elaborate a common point of view. One member of the small group, not the initial position taker, prepares a verbal summary of the small group's deliberations for the benefit of the larger group.

The facilitator asks all to return to their places in the original circle. The facilitator asks for brief reports from the small groups' spokespersons, and then calls on those who had a hard time deciding which voice to join to express their point of view. The facilitator then proceeds to solicit more—perhaps more well-considered—points of view from others, challenging participants to build on the reports from the smaller groups or just working on hunch about what people are really thinking but not yet saying. The aim is to push the discussion past superficial toward more heartfelt and strongly held position taking.

At the end of this second round of whole group discussion, the facilitator again identifies distinct voices and summarizes what those voices are saying. The facilitator asks the group to divide into new small groups along the lines of the voices just expressed. These new small groups elaborate what the voices mean, and report back to the whole group when the circle is reconstituted. If a high energy level can be sustained, three or even four rounds of large-group discussions followed by small-group elaboration may be desirable. The facilitator must gauge carefully along the way whether all who wish to have expressed their voices, and determine if increasing numbers in the group are being more forthright about their reactions to the original assertion.

After the last round, the facilitator captures on newsprint sheets the upshot of the multiple discussions. In doing this, it may be of value to memorialize voices expressed earlier as well as later. In addition, both bold individual points of view and collective strivings toward agreement are important to retain. The net result should be an accurate rendering of major areas of agreement and disagreement within the group.

Success Markers

In undertaking the exercise, the facilitator should think of himself or herself as a group writing implement, "a pencil with a brain." The purpose is to enable others to advance their points of view, to hear their colleagues' points of view, and to refine their own. The exercise is not intended as a platform for the facilitator to express his or her point of view about an issue. As the activity unfolds, the facilitator also serves as a sorter, batching like ideas and labeling the batches, thus highlighting areas of agreement and disagreement for group consideration. The exercise does not serve well as a device for imposing consensus on a group where one does not actually exist.

Finding a fit pace for the conduct of the exercise is essential. On the one hand, a facilitator can rush the process, not allowing participants enough time to express distinct and divergent points of view or small groups enough time to converse and prepare their reports. On the other hand, the facilitator can dawdle, eliciting too many individual positions or letting small group discussions become diffuse. The facilitator has to display enough of a sense of urgency to convince participants that there is good purpose to the deliberations without rushing them. Desired intensity, enthusiasm, and focus are present when there is high decibel level in small-group interchanges and participants position their bodies inward, toward the center of a discussion.

Refined observation and listening skills, and the ability to paraphrase group members' positions on the spot, are also essential for effective facilitation of Voices. The facilitator has to pick up on what constitutes a separate position worth designating as a voice. The facilitator then has to be able to frame five or so such positions well enough for participants to decide which voice magnetizes them. These capacities are crucial when moving to the second and third rounds of the exercise because the intent is to deepen the discussion, to get below and behind more readily expressed positions and uncover those that will influence members' decisions in a higher-stakes context.

Strategic Considerations

Voices requires an experienced facilitator. It should be undertaken only by those who can listen carefully to diverse perspectives, select the most salient ones, and encapsulate them on the spot. To have the greatest positive effect, it also requires groups made up of participants who can risk being forthright with each other and can manage and benefit from others' holding very different points of view. This is not to say that the exercise has little value for less seasoned groups. Quite the contrary, Voices is a useful device for collecting participant perspective in groups that have not worked together at all. It is just that the demands on the facilitator and the group are much greater when there is a consequential project underway, in contrast to a first-time gathering to share ideas and learn about each other's perspectives.

Questions for a Short Debrief of Voices

+ What did you glean from this exercise about areas of agreement and disagreement on the issue before you; perspectives you hold in common and ones you do not; the process of attaining greater forthrightness with each other; and your capacity to manage the differences among you?

+ What elements or aspects of the exercise do you want to incorporate into your repertoire of deliberative techniques? Which specifically will you do with your next set of deliberations, different from what you have done to date?

TUG OF WAR

Purposes

This exercise helps to sharpen differences of opinion within a group. At the same time, it assists a group in defining key terms that relate to its main task. Tug of War assumes the existence of conflict within a group and aims to surface it and reveal its contours, particularly the artful stratagems that participants use to defend their positions.

The exercise unfolds along the same lines as the playground game of the same name. The major difference is that instead of a rope for each side to pull on, there is a contention regarding a fundamental issue facing the group. The objective of the players nonetheless remains the same: to pull as many opponents as possible over to their side of the line.

Setup

No props are needed for the exercise, only a suitable work space allowing two sides to form and face each other, sitting or standing. The presence of an actual rope placed between the groups may be a helpful metaphor. The exercise consumes about an hour.

Instructions

To begin, the facilitator makes an assertion that is central to the work of the participants, one on which there is likely to be deep difference of opinion. Working recently with a group of emerging educational leaders, I asked them to divide over the following issue: that future school-restructuring efforts will require teachers to express more un-conditional love for their students because they are not receiving enough of it at home. One central concept—in the example given, unconditional love—is intended as the focus for controversy.

Having asked two opposing sides to form on the issue and align themselves on opposite sides of the room facing each other, the facilitator invites the contending forces to undertake a discussion. The facilitator explains that each side should do its best to convince the other of the merits of its position and the weaknesses of its opponents' position. The facilitator adds that at designated junctures in the discussion, participants will be asked if anyone wants to switch sides based on the arguments presented by their opponents. Whichever side winds up with the most people when the facilitator calls time—usually 20 minutes to a half hour—"wins."

Success Markers

Whether a group divides evenly or not on an issue at the outset is not consequential. The existence of uneven sides, in fact, tends to intensify the discussion more quickly. The shorthanded side sees itself as a hardy band of dissidents, whereas the larger considers itself a juggernaut on the brink of prevailing, thus making for some welcome fireworks.

With more even sides, discussion usually starts out haltingly, with tame arguments advanced by each side. After a few minutes, the facilitator can intervene and ask if anyone wants to shift sides. At this point, it is unlikely that anyone will. The facilitator suggests that both sides do not appear to be making very convincing arguments given that all are standing pat. This usually motivates participants to reach for more persuasive arguments and use seductive strategies to convince their opponents of the validity of their point of view.

After one or two more stoppages, someone usually breaks ranks and goes over to the other side. The facilitator can encourage this by saying something like, "A few of you appear to be nodding your heads in response to the others' arguments, yet you're not moving over. What's going on?" Finally, as the intensity of the discussion crests and appears to be waning, the facilitator halts the proceedings.

The back-and-forth that takes place in Tug of War should center on the meaning of key terms in the assertion presented. In the example offered above, promising signs include extensive exploration of what unconditional love means in context and the ramifications of attempting to create a locus for it in schools instead of or in addition to its place in the home. Mounting intensity in the pulling that develops between the two sides is also positive, in the form of more eloquent arguments and craftier attempts to draw the opposition across the line.

Strategic Considerations

Tug of War should be used when it is clear that a group will benefit from a vigorous contest centering on a critical issue facing it. Additionally, if it would be productive to see how different people in a group align on a certain question, it is probably time for a tug of war. A facilitator should, however, take into account that this activity surfaces and sharpens differences within a group. As with other exercises in this section on conflict management, Tug of War is likely to be of benefit only after solid team building has occurred.

In debriefing the exercise, the facilitator should focus on the following themes: the nature of the substantive differences regarding the identified issue; the dynamics of the interaction between the two "warring forces"; and the implications for the group's common understanding of and commitment to essential elements of its work, including vision and strategy.

Questions About What Happened

+ What is the essential difference in view between the two sides? Can you pin it down to one major area of disagreement?

+ On what do the two sides seem to agree? What is their common ground?

+ What were some of the more notable arguments and tactics that participants used to draw opponents over to their side? Did some work better than others? Which ones and why?

+ To what extent did discussants show flexibility in their position taking? Or alternatively, to what extent were they entrenched in their views?

Questions About Implications

+ What can you learn from this activity about your capacity as a group to find common ground on tough issues?

+ Which forces promote and reinforce your tendencies toward agreement? Which forces promote and reinforce your tendencies toward disagreement?

+ Do all tough issues inevitably produce a pull and tug within a group? Are all tough issues essentially "political footballs"?

+ What would have to be done to produce less contentious interaction? Would this be a good thing or a bad thing?

Questions About Applications

+ How does this exercise inform your thinking about the vision this group has for its work?

+ How does it inform your thinking about the strategies you have developed?

+ As you engage in further discussions of one sort or another, do you plan to do anything differently from what you did in this activity? Will you, for example, employ any new approaches or tactics with colleagues—attempt to be more persuasive in certain ways or more flexible in others?

LEADERS' WALK

Purposes

Organizations work best when leaders and followers work in concert. This exercise offers participants an opportunity to explore the leadership-followership connection, especially to attain a finer understanding of how tensions creep into the connection and affect all who are part of a project, and ultimately how much caring and thoughtfulness it takes to get around these tensions.

Setup

The exercise is best done outdoors where there is greater variation in terrain, including an array of natural obstacles, and potentially more freedom of movement for participants. It can, however, be done inside a building as long as there are enough passageways and empty rooms to provide a group with a relatively long and convoluted path. Well before beginning the exercise, the facilitator completes a reconnaissance of the route and makes note of obstacles such as rocks or chairs, streams or drains, low trees or narrow entryways, and other objects that may warrant careful guiding. It cannot be overemphasized that obstacles should be easily traversable by a person who may be overweight or have a bad back. Obstacles should in effect provoke curiosity, not personal injury. Blindfolds are the only necessary props. Normally the exercise consumes about an hour, including the debrief. Up to 25 people can participate as one group.

Instructions

The facilitator asks the group to stand and all to don blindfolds. The facilitator says that the group is going to take a guided walk together and that one of their number will remain sighted to assist them along the way. The facilitator reassures all that he or she will remain sighted and will accompany them on the walk to ensure that there are no unsafe moves. The facilitator also clarifies forms of allowable group communication. There are at least three the facilitator may choose from: 1) the activity will be conducted silently, with no talking by any participant until the debrief; 2) unsighted participants may talk with the participant who is sighted and vice versa, but unsighted participants may not talk with each other; or 3) all are free to talk with each other throughout the activity. Each of these three has its advantages.

The first compels leader and followers to develop modes of communication other than verbal, with only the former having the benefit of sight. The second focuses attention on the quality of verbal communication between leader and followers. The third is free flowing and open.

As participants are donning blindfolds, the facilitator also asks which one of them will remain sighted and thus become the leader. Discussion ensues and, more times than not, there is no ready consensus about who it should be. Naturally, who is chosen and why is a fertile topic for discussion afterward. If there is even mild disagreement within the group on the choice of leader, the facilitator can suggest that the group might want to start with one person and switch to another as the activity progresses. It is more desirable, I believe, to have someone as leader who has no formal authority in the group. This usually makes for less inhibited discussion of the leadership-followership dynamics in the debrief.

When the group is ready, the facilitator instructs the leader on roughly where to take the group and notes that there will be some obstacles to traverse or circumvent as they proceed. Finally, the facilitator suggests that the job of leader is to offer followers an intriguing journey while keeping them safe. Then off they go. After about 15 minutes of a guided walk, led by one or more of their number, participants reconvene and take off their blindfolds, and the debrief begins.

Success Markers

In addition to some of the suggestions offered in the section above, the facilitator should pay close attention to the communication systems the group develops. Of particular interest are the way messages are conveyed from the leader to those closest to him or her and from those nearby the leader to those farthest away. The articulation of needs and concerns on the part of followers and their effect on the leader's actions are also of import, especially if followers begin to grumble or express mild discontent. Finally, the balance that the leader effects between keeping charges safe against offering them a challenging journey is worth heeding.

Strategic Considerations

The placement of Leaders' Walk in a sequence should reflect sensitivity to its theme, the conflict associated with leadership-followership dynamics. Because participants are deprived of sight and perhaps verbal interaction, the exercise is probably best done after a group has developed modest levels of rapport and trust, when members are ready to confront tough issues together without fear of damaging each others' egos. The exercise bears most fruit if participants can safely express their frustrations with moving about unsighted and their dissatisfaction with the quality of the guidance they receive in the process.

Questions About What Happened

+ What were your reactions as followers to being led about? What was the hardest part for you? The easiest? The most unexpected element?

+ As a leader, what was your reactions to leading a group of people beset as they were with lack of sight and ability to converse? What was the hardest part for you? The easiest? The most unexpected element?

+ What did you do as followers to overcome your constraints? As a leader what did you do?

+ What sorts of systems did you develop, or on reflection wish you had? Especially communication systems to facilitate movement? Did you, for example, try to get some things straight with each other before starting out, or did you just take off? When things were not going as smoothly as they might have, did you caucus and try to make some corrections?

+ What was it like to be at a distance from the sighted person? I heard some grumbling from those of you who were out of range. What was that about?

Questions About Implications

+ What were the advantages and disadvantages of the communication and coordination systems you developed? How could you build on the advantages and downplay the disadvantages?

+ What did you learn about the requisites of effective leadership-followership interaction? Are there any special responsibilities of leaders that you can deduce from experiencing this activity? What about the special responsibilities of followers?

+ Was there any conflict that developed during the exercise? Inside you? Within the group? What were its roots? Its dynamics? How did the conflict arise? Unfold? Get resolved?

Questions About Applications

+ If you could insinuate one piece of learning from this exercise into your work, what would it be? What steps would you take to apply it?

+ Leaders and followers, whether formally designated or not, work under an array of constraints. They can overcome these constraints together, if they are savvy and thoughtful. Tell me one or two of the most significant constraints confronting leaders in your organization and detail the fledgling steps you might take to wriggle out of them or circumvent them. Now turn your attention to followers and do the same.

RITUAL CONFLICT

Purposes

This exercise is based on a much more extensive experience drawn from Native American lore called the Bone Game. A description of the Bone Game appears in an article written by Michael Brown in the May 1990 issue of the *Journal of Experiential Education*. The aim of Ritual Conflict is analogous to that of the Bone Game. In the main, it is to deepen participants' understanding of the roots of conflict, with particular emphasis on the forms it takes in organizations.

More than any other experience with which I am familiar, the exercise draws participants' attention to a core of concerns regarding conflict. A key assumption of the exercise is that conflict is inevitable, the result of a combination of misunderstandings and differences in values. The central question posed for participants is what they can do to eliminate unnecessary conflict and make the most out of the remainder that is unavoidable. Because the exercise promotes conflict through the establishment of two parallel and competing organizational cultures, participants can also derive rich perspective on the advantages of differing approaches to decision making and the difficulties of communication among organizational units.

Setup

The activity consumes at least 4 hours, and requires two meeting spaces far enough apart to leave questions in participants' minds about where the other group is meeting. It works best with groups of between 16 and 24, that is, two subgroups of between 8 and 12 each. Before the day set for the exercise, the facilitator instructs participants to bring with them an object of autobiographical significance, something that has more intrinsic than extrinsic value and expresses something important about their background (Illustration 5.3).

Prior to the start of the exercise, the facilitator randomly divides the whole group into two working subgroups. That this be done randomly is important. Every other name on an alphabetized list, with only minor adjustments perhaps to even up men and women, is one way. Evening up on racial or ethnic grounds is possible, but less desirable. It can cause unnecessary distortions in the debrief afterward, detracting from the main thrusts of the exercise, which focus on communication, decision making, and conflict management.

Illustration 5.3.

Instructions

At the very beginning of the exercise, the facilitator guides the two subgroups to their separate work spaces, first one and then the other. To a greater or lesser extent, the two are meant to be unaware of the other's whereabouts. The facilitator hands out to each subgroup sets of directions (reprinted in Chart 5.1) and asks if there are any questions—yet answers as few as possible. The facilitator notes where the bathrooms are and says that from here on in, "When I am in the room, treat me as invisible." Then the facilitator invites the participants to go to work.

Success Markers

Countless phenomena from the activity present themselves as talking points. Successful learning is assured if two things happen: First, the facilitator becomes invisible almost immediately and lets the groups get underway, taking as much time as they wish and performing their assigned tasks in the order they feel appropriate; and second, the facilitator organizes the debrief so as to manage the unwieldy number of talking points that will undoubtedly emerge. One knows that the exercise is on its way to success if the debrief is so engaging that the participants themselves decide to forego a planned break to continue discussing the activity. The main challenge in the debrief is to help participants make a transition from dwelling on who did what to whom to analyzing objectively what happened and determining how to factor their learning into their future work with each other.

Strategic Considerations

Ritual Conflict can produce some hard feelings. Because the two groups tend to attribute negative intent to each other, tensions will almost certainly emerge between the groups. In light of this, the exercise should be inserted only after a group has engaged in substantial team building. Group cohesion will help deflect the splitting and distancing that may occur in the wake of the activity. At the same time, the conflict that arises will illuminate contrasting modes of group functioning, and if handled correctly, will impel participants to think hard and learn some important things. Although total group harmony will assuredly be tested by Ritual Conflict, it will likely be much stronger afterward than it was before.

For this exercise, I have not attempted to roll out a long list of questions. Rather, I have sought to focus attention on major areas of questioning, leaving to facilitators the task of framing their own hand-crafted questions. The reason is that the exercise provides such rich material that there are literally thousands of questions that might be posed. The best service I can provide here is to ensure that no major area of potential learning is overlooked.

Normally it makes sense for the debrief to take place on the day after the exercise, to allow participants time to reflect, perhaps to do some initial concept development, perhaps just to get over some initial stewing. It may also be useful to ask participants at the very end of the activity to prepare for the debrief by writing up a short list of events, issues, or one-liners they would like to discuss. There is likely to be significant overlap between the matters they raise and the areas listed below. But be careful to heed the points of view participants express and be prepared to help the group wrestle with them.

As participants arrive for the debrief, invite them to write their proposed talking points on a blackboard or on newsprint. Then ask the participants to divide again into the groups with which they worked, on opposite sides of the room. The facilitator should dedicate a considerable amount of time at the outset to having participants unburden themselves regarding what happened in the activity and how they feel about what happened. If the facilitator attempts to move on prematurely to implications or applications, the group may balk. Still immersed in feelings about what happened, participants will be unlikely to agree to discussing generalizations of any sort.

CHART 5.1. Directions for Ritual Conflict

Begin by telling others in the group the biographical significance of the object you brought in. When all have done this, the objects should be passed around in a circle for all to view, handle, and ponder. When every object has been circulated to every participant in your group, the process of selecting one to represent the power of voice in the group begins. This is done by recirculating the objects again among all, this time in silence. You are empowered to set aside any object, your own or someone else's. The objects continue circulating until there is only one that remains. This becomes the representation of your group's voice.

Your group should now proceed to identify a name for itself. Discussion on this and all subsequent matters takes place as follows: Only the person who has the object of group voice in his or her possession can speak; the one whose object it is begins all discussions and passes it to another participant only when he or she is finished speaking. All decisions are made by consensus: Specifically, a participant with the object in hand makes a formal proposal and all others can vote yea or nay or can abstain. Only those votes without any nays represent decisions of the group. If there are nays on any matter, those participants who so voted, can express, if they wish, the reason for their negative vote. No proposal can come before the group more than two times in which there been one or more negative votes cast.

Following the determination of name, the group then chooses from among its members people to perform the following three roles: spokesperson, aide, and gambler. The spokesperson represents the position of the group to the other group by verbally negotiating with the spokesperson of that group. He or she must be faithful to the decisions his or her group makes. The aide accompanies the spokesperson to the negotiations with the other group, but has no voice other than to confer off to the side with the spokesperson. The aide's main role is to report back to the group what transpired in negotiations and to assist with further strategy development. The gambler represents his or her group in a game of chance that takes place with the other group to determine who wins the stakes.

The last of the two groups' initial decisions involves the establishment of stakes they are willing to put up in a wager with the other group. The stakes should be real but not excessive, something of value to the subgroup that, if lost, would cause inconvenience or difficulty to the members. Refreshments, symbolic gestures, and services are possibilities.

Having made these decisions, the spokesperson and aide emerge from their group's meeting room in search of the other group's spokesperson and aide. Eventually they engage them and begin negotiations regarding stakes and terms that will govern the conduct of the game of chance that will decide which group wins the stakes. All, repeat ALL, items of concern to either group are open to negotiation between the two groups through their respective spokespersons and aides.

If, before time expires, the groups are ready to play the game of chance and decide a winner, the facilitator provides them with two small objects, one of which is worth a point, the other of which has no value. A penny and a dime will do. The game is played as follows: One group's gambler hides the two objects, one in each hand; the other group's gambler points to the closed hand he or she wants to see opened. The winner is the group that attains 5 points first. Again, all matters are negotiable, including which group's gambler hides first, which points first, and whether the gambler who does not point first receives a final turn before the game concludes.

Areas for Discussion of What Happened

+ During the activity, what were you thinking the other group was up to?

+ Talk about what it was like to function in the mode of consensus decision making that the exercise demanded.

+ You had to make decisions about matters such as group object, group name, roles, and stakes. What were some of the other key decisions your group made?

+ At point of first contact between the spokespersons, what exactly happened? Step by excruciating step, what unfolded? Who did what and at what points in this initial interchange did they do it?

+ Was there conflict between the two groups? What was it about?

+ Discuss how you felt about finishing the activity, that is, getting to play the game of chance? Was it an imperative or not for your group?

+ What happened in the negotiations? Between the two spokespersons in particular, what exactly went on?

+ Talk about the relationship of the two groups, especially as it developed over the time the spokespersons and aides conducted their negotiations.

Areas for Discussion of Implications

+ From your reflections on this activity, what did you learn about communication and decision making in organizations? What about communication and decision making in work groups or teams? What about between groups that have to interact with each other to get something done that involves both of them?

+ If there was conflict between the groups, what were its roots, its origins, its sources?

+ What were its dynamics, its evolution, its flow?

+ How important is point of first contact between groups in organizations?

+ What did you learn about the process of negotiating, that is, two groups attempting to get things through designated representatives?

Areas for Discussion of Applications

+ Identify specific measures you need to incorporate into your work with each other to avoid needless conflict.

+ Identify specific measures you need to adopt to manage conflict to your advantage rather than letting its disadvantages take hold.

+ Identify systems you need to develop to manage conflict appropriately.

Exercises on Using Diversity

Introduction

Unjustified stereotypes that people carry about other people are a major block to organizational progress. Just getting along is not good enough. Staff have to be treated fairly, and differing perspectives have to be appreciated before an organization can do the same for clients and customers. These are some of the maxims that increasingly govern the operations of organizations in all sectors. It is generally accepted dogma that to be productive, organizations must capitalize on the diversity of the people that work for them. Yet, real progress on this front has been hard to achieve. This is despite the fact that there is broad coverage of the subject of diversity by a host of consultants and trainers as well as a wide array of print and video training packages.

If the challenge of using diversity in organizations has not been met—and I think most would agree it has not—a principal reason is that most of the treatments deployed are flawed in the approach they take to the learner. They are for the most part didactic, which is to say that they preach to the "unconverted." Workshops and training packages do this in two ways, and as a result fail to avail participants of the room they need for personal growth. First, they provide participants with a ready-made definition of diversity, either explicitly or implicitly, and ask them to accept it for purposes of self-improvement. Usually the definition is a relatively legalistic one, having to do with race, ethnicity, gender, religion, and perhaps sexual orientation. Rarely do offerings and materials invite participants to create a sense of what diversity means to them. The point here is a simple one, that a person is much more likely to want to come to terms with a problem if he or she has a substantial role in defining what its dimensions are.

The second flaw relates to the first. Accompanying a preset definition of diversity is a standard of behavior that participants assume, quite rightly, that the designers of the training do not believe they meet. The natural response of the participants is either quiet resentment or vociferous denial, but in any case, the upshot is that they are defensive. Their personal identity has been threatened. Rarely is learning possible under such circumstances.

The exercises in this section serve as a platform for participants to make personal meaning with regard to diversity. They provide a relatively unthreatening environment in which participants can experiment with a modification of attitudes. The exercises do not preach, nor do they inherently cause defensiveness. Instead, they provide participants an opportunity to discern more clearly their own backgrounds in relation to their colleagues'. Mapping Diversity and Diversity Bingo, for example, are fit entry points for participants to begin to define diversity in their own terms. Listening in More Than One Voice and Stereotyping honor the existence of people's different perspectives and show participants how they can increase their own effectiveness by taking others' positions and backgrounds into account. The Being invites participants to find common meaning regarding what they believe is essential for a group to use diversity to its advantage.

Although these exercises point in the right direction on the matter of using diversity, they are admittedly only initial cuts into a difficult and complex task. Hardly a solution, they nonetheless have more potential than most of what is on the market today. They grant participants space rather than cornering them, and as a result encourage movement based more on self-reflection than on self-recrimination.

MAPPING DIVERSITY

Purposes

Mapping Diversity, or more simply the Map, is about the places that people come from. As such, it helps to uncover some of their history and perspective and how these affect their thinking. It is also an exercise about listening to and absorbing important information about other peoples' backgrounds and serves as a fit preface for working more effectively with them.

Setup

The exercise requires a relatively large open space in which participants can move about freely. A lawn or other open area will do quite well. Inside, a cleared space the size of a classroom or a dining area that otherwise would have been occupied by tables will suffice. Group size dictates how large an area is required. Although there is no limit to how many people can benefit from the exercise, a smaller, more intimate group of about 20 to 25 is ideal. I have done the exercise with groups as large as 300. With smaller groups, the exercise takes roughly half an hour. It may take longer with larger contingents. Understand that if there are a host of participants, the polling process described below can tap only a sample of participant responses, or the experience will become quite tedious.

Treating the chosen space as a piece of topography, the facilitator simulates the boundaries of an area, a state, the continental United States, or possibly even a global region—whatever seems most appropriate for the group in question. Simulation is accomplished easily by the use of markings similar to ones that children might lay out for a pick-up game. "The red shirt is Maine, the chair southern California, the book bag Seattle, and the empty cups Key West." A similar process can be followed for areas other than the continental United States. Illustration 6.1 offers one perspective.

The facilitator prepares for the activity by framing a set of queries for participants, usually three or four in toto. All the questions are about places on the map that have past or future meaning for the participants. Examples are "Where on the map did you have your best meal ever?" or "Where did you go to high school?" Taken together, the questions should show a progression from the introductory and lighthearted to ones demanding more background information and relating more directly to the group's task.

Illustration 6.1.

First questions seek pieces of information that participants are unlikely to know about each other, but, when known, are normally viewed as welcome information by fellow participants. The locale and kind of high school a person attended is one such tidbit. A more demanding question is where on the map a person acquired useful preparation for the work the group will do together. If, for example, the work entails building a personnel information system, a fit question might be to ask about the spot on the map where a participant overlooked an essential dimension of the people he or she was working with and as a result was brought up short. The key is the framing and phrasing of the questions and the establishment of an order that goes from innocuous but interesting to serious and substantively relevant.

Instructions

The facilitator begins the exercise by asking the participants to stand. The facilitator explains that he or she wants them to imagine a map on the floor, or the lawn, of the United States, or Michigan, and he or she points out the boundary markers for the entity chosen. The facilitator then explains that he or she will be asking participants to go to a series of places on the map that respond to questions he or she will pose. When they arrive at their "destination" in response to a particular question, they should look around, see who is nearby, and engage in a moment of small talk about people's exact whereabouts. After a few seconds of chatter, the facilitator quiets everyone and polls the group one by one about where they are standing. Undoubtedly, some will offer explanation or perhaps show pride. There will be a titter if, for example, two people who had worked together for a while had in fact attended the same high school and were not aware of it until this point.

The facilitator then asks a second question. Participants move to the place on the map that represents their response. This time, after the chatter dies down, the facilitator asks not only where each person is standing but why or how he or she got there or what happened there. On the third round, assuming that the facilitator's question provokes more thought and leads to slightly more revelation on the part of participants, the polling process takes longer. Participants' explanations are fuller and more on point with the challenge before the group.

Success Markers

Vigorous chatter and enthusiasm are the most important indicators that the activity is working well. In the latter stages of questioning, the facilitator has to ensure that the reporting by participants does not become tedious. Their responses tend to become longer and more detailed as the questions become more demanding.

Strategic Considerations

The Map is almost always used as a lead-off exercise with a group. It helps those who are not well acquainted get to know each other. It also helps those who think they know each other well learn some new things. The exercise overtly fulfills the desire "to know where someone else is coming from." It sets the stage for further work and provokes discussion of issues best discussed early on in the life cycle of group work.

Questions

There are two major paths one can pursue in debriefing the Map. The first involves an examination of the character and diversity of the group. Sample questions include, Are you a diverse group? In what ways are you diverse? Diverse as to background? How so? Diverse in the way you approach problems, face challenges, right mistakes, handle conflict? How so?

Regarding this first path, I learned early on in using the Map not to underestimate the value of seemingly innocuous information gathered from an activity that is introductory. I once used the Map with a group composed of business leaders, government officials, and environmental advocates. They had been brought together to search for agreement on ways to preserve the quality of the natural resources in four northern Michigan counties. My first question was where they all went to high school. The sole intent I had in asking it was to encourage greater mutual understanding within the group of the backgrounds of its individual members. In response to the question, everyone in the room except one, a farmer from near Traverse City, moved to the part of the map denoting the Detroit area. There was considerable surprise on everyone's part that nearly all the invested parties who would be working to preserve a piece of rural northern Michigan had grown up in the Detroit suburbs. A useful bit of demographic data!

This first path, the posing of questions in an open-response mode, also reveals how well people listen to what others say. Granted, the activity is meant to be a "pop quiz" rather than a "blue book examination." Yet it is possible to discern from the quality and richness of observations offered in the debrief how well individuals listened to information others provided. Further, one can also learn who in the group has the ability to patch together multiple and diverse bits of information into a coherent picture.

The second possible path entails issuing a challenge rather than asking questions. The facilitator asks the group to form four diverse groups on the spot based on the information gathered from responses to the questions posed in the activity. In all likelihood, some participants will immediately ask what exactly is meant by "diverse." The facilitator readily responds, "However you construe it, based on what you just learned about each other." After some milling about, the subgroups finally form. The facilitator then asks why participants divided themselves as they did, that is, which dimensions of diversity they took into account to form the diverse groups.

My experience is that this relatively simple maneuver can yield some memorable insights for both facilitator and participants. One humorous example: An African American man, part of a group of educators I was working with, reported in the debrief following the formation of diverse subgroups that he was initially wondering which of the four he should join. As his eyes quickly scanned the room, he realized that there were only three other African Americans present. So he blurted out, "I guess I won't be in the same group as any of my brothers." With this aside, he provided a great service to all in the room, cutting below the surface on the issue of racial representation, a critical concern that this group had to address. It might easily have remained unaddressed for the entirety of the time we worked together were it not for this one candid observation.

DIVERSITY BINGO

Purposes

Diversity Bingo invites participants to understand the extent to which they themselves stereotype others solely on the basis of superficial characteristics. It also introduces members of a group to the dimensions of diversity that exist within the group.

Setup

The main prop in the exercise is a specially designed bingo card, an example of which is provided in Chart 6.1. Note that the card has 25 cells. Each includes a statement about what a given person has done or knows how to do, or where a person is from. The activity works best with groups that exceed 15 because larger numbers provide a broader base of respondents to the multiple questions posed on the card.

The action, knowledge, or background elements in each cell varies according to the experience level of the participants with whom one is working. The facilitator has to adapt the card accordingly. For one group, it may make little sense to insert a cell about having attended a "Take Back the Night" rally, for another, knowing how to do regression analysis. In toto, however, the cells should include an array of elements that pertain to predominant concerns such as discrimination on the basis of race, gender, and so on. They should also include a few elements whose meaning only one or two in a group will grasp.

The cells on the card should not describe participants' characteristics per se. Note, for example, the one regarding familiarity or experience with a handicap condition; it does not say "a person who is handicapped." It refers instead to "a person who has played a wheelchair sport." The aim here is not political correctness, but to broach issues of difference among people by focusing on the more matter-of-fact areas of doing, knowing, and being as opposed to characterizations that cast a wide and stigmatizing net over large numbers of people. The phrasing should model, in a modest way, the kind of restraint that might take the edge out of human relations in general. Keeping to what others know and do in interactions is usually more beneficial than focusing on what they are like.

One of the more controversial cells in the example is the one that asks about knowing a person who uses food stamps. Note that it does not ask directly if the respondent uses food stamps, but adds a buffer

CHART 6.1. Diversity Bingo Card

Person who has served meals in a soup kitchen. _____	Person who has milked a cow. _____	Person who knows how to do regression analysis. _____	Person who has more than one set of step-siblings or stepchildren. _____	Person who has attended a "Take Back the Night" rally. _____
Person who has overcome a disability. _____	A single parent. _____	Person who shared a home meal with a family of a different race. _____	Person who has lived more than 5 years in a town of less than 2,000. _____	Person who is first college grad in his or her nuclear family. _____
Person who knows someone who uses food stamps. _____	Person who has prayed at a mosque. _____	Person who speaks two or more languages. _____	Person who has done bungi jumping. _____	Person who has played a wheelchair sport. _____
Person born in an Asian country. _____	Person who has dated someone of a different race. _____	A single child. _____	Male with paid child care experience. _____	Person who has run for political office. _____
Person who rode a city bus to and from work or school. _____	Female who has worked on a construction crew. _____	Person who has lived in another country for 2 or more years. _____	Person who has two or more living grandparents. _____	Person who has attended a Bar or Bat Mitzvah. _____

between respondent and act. The reasoning here is that even a light-hearted exercise, when it encompasses matters of diversity, can engender bad feeling. I myself once used a card that had a cell titled "person who uses food stamps." In the debrief that followed the activity, an African American woman noted that a stream of people had approached her and asked if she could fill in that cell. In fact she could not, but the tension that was produced in the ensuing discussion of the matter stretched my capacity as a facilitator. The strength of feelings in the room was palpable, and caused me to back off on such matters, resolving that with groups just getting to know each other, I would proceed with a little more caution.

Instructions

To begin the exercise, the facilitator provides each participant with a card and then asks all to stand up. A sufficient amount of floor space is needed so that participants can mill about asking each other questions relating to the items in the cells on the bingo card. The facilitator carefully explains that getting bingo is the aim and that the way to do this is to secure the names of other people in the room in five cells on the card, up and down, across or diagonally, but all in a straight line.

It is important for the facilitator to note that askers must pose a specific question to a colleague, for example, "Are you a person who . . . ?" They are not allowed to approach another person and ask if he or she can "fill in one of the cells." After several minutes, someone blurts out "Bingo!" The facilitator congratulates the winner, and perhaps awards a small gift.

A short aside. The facilitator should not assume that all in a group know what Bingo is. I had my own lesson on diversity when I made this error and was brought up short by two Korean participants who looked at me oddly as I initiated the activity.

Success Markers

Hubbub is good. When it starts to die down, it is time for the debrief. It is important to keep the debrief as lighthearted as the activity itself, granting that there may be tinges of seriousness, particularly if some participants say they experienced some stereotyping in the questions asked them or some nervousness about asking others certain kinds of questions.

Strategic Considerations

Diversity Bingo works best when inserted at the beginning of a group task. Like Mapping Diversity, it offers participants the opportunity to get some data about who else is in the room, what their backgrounds are, what they may or may not have done and know about, and how they think about themselves. It is unlikely to be very useful for a group in the middle of its assignment.

There are relatively few questions for the facilitator to pose to the group after it has completed the activity. But each question should provoke answers from a number of people, and those answers can provide the means for a group to understand better the challenges of using diversity in organizations.

Questions About What Happened

+ Any questions posed to you as a respondent that surprised you?

+ Any questions posed to you as a respondent that did not surprise you at all, but, rather, that you would have expected?

+ Which of the questions gave you pause as you thought about asking them of others in the group? Which caused you some discomfort as you thought about asking them?

+ Which of the questions in the cells did you not know the full meaning of?

Questions About Implications and Applications

+ Given what a number of you have just said, do you have any summary observations about the diversity of this group? How diverse are you? In what ways?

+ Given what you have just said, what are you as a group saying that diversity entails?

+ Do you have some observations about the ease or difficulty with which you as a group approach matters of diversity? Are you comfortable being frank and open with each other about matters of diversity? Are you less comfortable than you would like to be?

+ How would you gauge your capacity to manage matters of diversity in this group?

+ What are the implications for your capacity to manage matters of diversity within the larger organizational context in which you are working?

+ What things might you consider doing to upgrade your overall capacity to deal more effectively with matters of diversity as you have defined them here?

THE BEING

Purposes

The Being helps a group gain a deeper understanding of and appreciation for the diversity of its members and suggests how it might take advantage of this diversity. The exercise does this in an ostensibly innocuous way by inviting participants to reach consensus on a set of ideas about diversity and then to render the ideas in the form of a drawing on newsprint. The "being" in effect becomes a living embodiment of the group's diversity, including attributes that are easy to see as well as those that are not. The point the exercise brings out is that human diversity is organic and dynamic, like beings themselves, and it comprises aspects that are more subtle than race, gender, and ethnicity.

Setup

The exercise can be accomplished with groups of up to 25, and takes about an hour. The only props needed are newsprint and magic markers.

Instructions

To begin, the facilitator divides the group into subgroups totaling about five participants each, and provides each subgroup with newsprint sheets and magic markers. The task of the subgroups is to discuss and then list on newsprint the most notable dimensions of the whole group's diversity as they see them. After completing this task, they then generate ideas among themselves about which representative life form, for example, an animal, a plant, or some combination, best captures the dimensions on their list. When they have arrived at one that contains the essence of what is on the list, they make a simple sketch of it on newsprint.

The several subgroups then reconvene to share both their lists of dimensions and their rough sketches. A discussion ensues among the whole group on the dimensions taken together and the most fitting graphic representation of them. The facilitator's role is to help the group surface all that diversity means to it. The facilitator does this by pushing participants to struggle with the relational dynamics between the attributes of the beings they chose and dimensions of diversity. Evergreens overtaking beeches, antelopes locking horns, interlocking amino acid molecules—what do these have to with diversity in the human relationship?

The aim is for the whole group to arrive at one being that comprehends the ideas expressed. This may be difficult to accomplish in a single large-group discussion. Thus, the subgroups may need to reconvene in the wake of an initial get-together to modify their perspectives and meld them with those of their colleagues. The whole three-part process is captured in Illustration 6.2.

When there is enough of a consensus, the facilitator commissions a small team to render the being on about six newsprint sheets taped together. It may also be appropriate to annotate the drawing with words and expressions, using material from the lists developed by the subgroups.

Success Markers

The Being offers safe ground for the expression of ideas within a group about a topic that can be delicate. When going well, the activity should have a feel to it that resembles freeing up, ease of expression, emotional safety. Rarely do so-called diversity workshops carry an air of lightness; the Being should.

Strategic Considerations

The Being is more profitable for a group that has been through a series of experiential exercises, and thus has learned to appreciate the value of metaphor in illuminating aspects of its work. If a group is likely to see the Being as aimless child's play, it will probably not produce positive results. If, on the other hand, a group is ready to understand that comparative representations can gently clarify issues that are difficult to confront head on, then the exercise should bear fruit. As with all the exercises presented here, the debriefing of the experience solidifies the learning.

Illustration 6.2.

Questions About What Happened

+ What aspects of diversity were on your lists? Do they fall into categories? What are some of the categories?

+ How did you reach consensus about a being that best fits the dimensions of diversity as you viewed them? What were the more prominent decision points in the deliberations that led to your choosing a being? What ideas or notions were discarded as you went through this process?

Questions About Implications and Applications

+ What did you learn about the diversity of your group? What did you learn about the way this group thinks about issues of diversity?

+ What will you do with your drawing? Toss it? Save it? Of what use is it?

+ Given the task(s) confronting your group, what will you do differently based on what you learned here? Did the activity help you identify particular attributes that you might consider using for particular purposes? What are they, and how would you suggest they be deployed?

LISTENING IN MORE THAN ONE VOICE

Purposes

This exercise increases participants' understanding of the diverse perspectives that can be brought to bear on an issue. Because it asks participants to adopt others' points of view, it compels active listening and encourages more effective communication among people from different backgrounds. One of its major assets is that it can be used in conjunction with any form of traditional presentation, such as a live or videotaped speech on a topic relating to the work of a group.

This case in point may help: A local firm is faced with what to do about significant demographic changes in its customer base. Top management has engaged an expert to analyze the situation and apprise all managers of the emerging trends and cite implications for the firm's work. A group from the marketing department has been assigned responsibility for identifying strategies to deal with these trends and recommending changes to top management.

Listening in More Than One Voice ensures that all members of the marketing group absorb what the expert has to say. It also enables more effective use on their part of the ideas presented. It does this by generating vigorous discussion not only of the content of the presentation but of the differing perceptions various listeners have of the content. The latter is especially important because marketing is concerned as much with perceptions as it is with the objective conditions.

Setup

Listening in More Than One Voice takes roughly an hour and requires no props.

Instructions

Here are the instructions the facilitator provides in advance of the expert presentation.

As you listen to this presentation, you are going to adopt an additional "listening voice." Obviously, you will listen carefully in your own voice. But I want you to select one of the following voices to listen in as well: a senior citizen, a Latina mom, an African American young man, a woman professional, a member of the Christian Coalition. Each of you should select a different voice, one that you see as different from your own. When we convene after the presentation, we will have a sequence of discussions. In our first discussion, you will contribute using your adopted voices. Then we will discuss the presentation with you using your own voices.

(Note that the voices above encompass demographic categories. Facilitators have to use their imaginations to tailor the list of possible voices to coincide with the group's mission.) The presentation occurs, and following it the discussions get underway. After the first discussion, the facilitator asks the participants to guess the adopted voice of each of their colleagues.

Success Markers

The facilitator should strongly encourage participants to engage actively with the role-play. If, in the first discussion, participants lose themselves in their adopted voices, the exercise is on the way to a fruitful outcome. I have seen this happen. Some participants actually forget that their colleagues are interpreting the presentation in their adopted rather than their own voice. Stimulating interaction is the result.

Strategic Considerations

The exercise can be deployed at any time in conjunction with a substantive presentation. It can be useful in the beginning, middle, or final stages of a group project. It should not, however, be used frivolously—only when there is solid justification such as that offered in the example above. A facilitator has to be able to say to himself or herself that this is a time when pushing people outside the boundaries of their way of looking at things would be exceedingly helpful; or alternatively, that this is a presentation whose contents must be absorbed and used for the group to fulfill its charge.

Questions

The debrief following the discussions should be brief and focus on questions such as these:

+ What was it like to listen to the presentation in two voices? Were you able to do it? What was easy? What was not?

+ What were the effects of listening to the presentation in two voices? The effects on your perspective regarding the material presented? The effects on your ability to absorb the material presented?

+ Compare the two discussions you had after the presentation. Which was more substantive and consequential, the one where you were role-playing or the one where you were not? Regarding the latter discussion, do you believe it would have been of the same quality if it had been the only one held, rather than one that took place in the wake of another where people had to interpret things through adopted voices?

+ What are the organizational applications of this exercise, if any? Are there activities you should do regularly that are analogous to Listening in More Than One Voice?

STEREOTYPES

Purposes

This is an exercise that shows how unwarranted stereotypes, when they are given full vent, disable group discussion and undermine organizational productivity. Stereotypes offers little indication at the outset that it concerns factors such as race, ethnicity, gender, and age. Yet the debrief, if done well, solidly confirms these connections. The fun of doing the exercise softens participants' potential defensiveness regarding the negative power of stereotyping. Stereotypes embeds the effects of the "before" state in participants' bodies and minds and then calls on them to create the "after" state.

Setup

The exercise works best if done with discussion groups of no more than 12. One facilitator can easily manage the setup for and oversight of the activity and joint debrief for up to three separate groups. Props include labels and headbands, one each per participant. 3 × 5 cards or pieces of shirt cardboard will do for the former, sweatbands or rolled up bandannas for the latter. The facilitator prints on each of the cards a designation of one to three words. Examples include "wise old hand," "incompetent," "untrustworthy," "team player," "victim," "good ol' boy or gal," "peacemaker," "divisive force." It is important to have roughly equal numbers of positive and negative designations among those chosen. Each person in a discussion group receives a different label. Duplicate sets of labels can be used with different discussion groups. About an hour should be set aside for the exercise, including debrief.

Instructions

The facilitator asks the groups to form separate discussion circles. Whether or not they sit at tables is inconsequential. The facilitator asks the participants to don their headbands and then moves about each of the circles placing a different label in the headband of each participant. All the discussants in a circle except the one wearing a given label are able to read what that particular label says.

When all participants are "labeled," the facilitator asks the group to undertake a discussion on a topic that relates to the task before them. My experience is that topics that call for a tangible product from the group work best. Developing an agenda of a 1-day conference to showcase findings relating to the principal project is one that has worked for me. Finally, the facilitator asks the participants, as they pursue their discussion, to honor the labels their colleagues are wearing. They should, in effect, treat each person according to his or her label.

Success Markers

Discussion ensues among the group or groups, although haltingly at first. The role-play is frustrating for some, rewarding albeit slightly confusing for others, but generally hilarious for most. One or two may show pique at having everything they say dismissed. Others may preen a bit at having everything they say adopted as gospel. After about 20 minutes, or whenever the intensity of the discussion begins to wane, the facilitator calls time and sets the stage for the debrief. To do this, the facilitator asks participants to see if, one after the other around the circle, they can guess what their label says before they themselves look at it. When all have had a shot at guessing and looking, the debrief begins. The exercise is on its way to fulfilling its purpose if, in the debrief, frivolity is transformed into serious discussion of unfair labeling and its deleterious consequences.

Strategic Considerations

Stereotypes as an activity can produce considerable gaiety in the early going. It can also can cause mild frustration and touches of anger in some participants. The debrief normally turns to a serious examination of the effects of stereotyping and how best to combat them. Some of this can be rather delicate as participants make linkages between personal inclinations and factors of race, ethnicity, gender, religion, and age; for example, women are overly emotional, African American people are unreliable, Jewish people are pushy, older people are wiser. For these reasons, the exercise should be inserted in a sequence only after substantial team building has taken place and other preliminary exercises on diversity have been accomplished.

Questions About What Happened

+ What was it like to conduct a group discussion under the constraints imposed by this exercise? What were the effects on you as group, and on you as individuals?

+ How much did you accomplish on the task you were given, that is, did you come up with a good outline of an agenda for the proposed 1-day conference?

+ Was it difficult, or easy, to carry out the role-play? Did you resist or adapt readily, to the routine of treating other participants according to their labels? How did you experience being stereotyped? How did you react to stereotyping others?

Questions About Implications

+ If you were not as productive as a group as you wanted to be, to what do you attribute this lack of productivity?

+ If your progress was confounded by the labeling, what do you make of this? Does anything like what happened in the activity go on in real meetings in real organizations? What form does labeling take in these contexts?

+ What if the relatively innocuous labels you were asked to wear in this exercise were in fact linked up with more immutable characteristics such as race, ethnicity, gender, or age? Are the effects experienced in the exercise analogous to ones experienced in the real world, where race, ethnicity, gender and age labeling is a daily occurrence? What are the parallels as you see them?

+ Labeling goes on all the time, and all of us engage in it. In many respects, it helps us get group work done because we know who is good at something and who is not so good at something else. What is the difference between helpful and harmful labeling? Can you make distinctions here? Can they be articulated so that organizations can promote the helpful over the harmful?

Questions About Applications

✦ What can you do to deflect the negative effect of labeling on your deliberations? In the short run? In the long run?

✦ Should you establish certain ground rules for this area that would impose responsibility on members of your group, not just the ones that are unfairly labeled, to call attention to labeling that is likely to cause a slowdown or setback in the work at hand?

✦ What kind of help could you use from outside your group to do a better job of managing the challenges here?

CHAPTER 7

The Exercises in Play: A Story of Real Organizational Change

Introduction

This is a tale of organizational development in action. It covers the four principal stages of an outside consultant's involvement with an organization: *engagement, entry, endeavor,* and *ending*. Its intent is to demonstrate the promise and potential as well as the frustration and challenge involved in a commitment to experiential forms of leadership development.

Engagement is the first interaction between consultant and client, resulting in either a meeting of the minds or a parting of the ways. Entry is the set of actions that allows a consultant to establish a viable role in the host organization. Endeavor is the actual work consultant and client do together over a specified period. Ending is how a consultant recedes from the host organization, leaving behind, more or less, organizational capacity in his or her wake. The story told here is an experiential composite, drawn from a few of my recent projects with different organizations.

Engagement, a Chancy Proposition

A potential client, the head of a large agency, contacted me and asked if I would be interested in assisting with an effort to improve the capacity of her top managers to function as a lead team within the organization. In an initial conversation, we exchanged basic information and perspectives—facts about the agency and about my qualifications to assist, basic data about the present context and conditions of the organization, and the general approach I would take in helping with the challenge at hand.

There were signs of growing enthusiasm on both sides, so we agreed to proceed to a more serious level. In our second conversation a few days later, I matter-of-factly inserted the idea that an integral part of the assistance I provide clients is well-placed experiential exercises. It was here that the shadow of divergence loomed. The offhand reference provoked a short silence between us, followed by a discernible intake of air by the client. Recovering composure, she put words to her pause: "What do you mean by experiential exercises?" Before responding, I too took a short breath, thinking to myself that we had reached the crux point of our interchange, the outcome of which would dictate whether we would move to the next phase, negotiation of initial terms, or decide to go our separate ways.

The following interchange mirrors the one we had and captures the progressive dynamic that developed between us.

Consultant: I work from a repertoire of about 50 exercises developed over the years. They are simulations that serve as so-called safe ground for the participants, allowing them to get away from the high-stakes interactions that confront them on the job. The exercises provide a place for people to experiment personally and professionally with new approaches. They pose familiar challenges in unfamiliar yet nonthreatening ways so that people can try on change before having to wear it.

Client: That sounds interesting, but can you tell me a bit more about these exercises, can you give me an example or perhaps describe how one would work?

Here I try to hide the big gulp of air I'm taking in, because I know the conversation has reached ground zero. Passing through my mind is a version of how some early devotees of management simulations saw this predicament.

So we invite people to participate. After they experience a simulation, they agree that our description is accurate. But now their problem is akin to ours; they do not know how to transmit to others what they have experienced in a way that expresses the essence of what they have learned, nor the excitement of what they felt. (Stumpf & Dutton, 1990, p. 7)

Consultant (*despite the inevitable stumbling block, I proceed confidently*): Sure, let me describe one where we focus on how members of a work group learn the benefits of mutually supporting each other through difficult challenges. I am talking particularly about the kind of support that enhances the parts played by individuals seeking to make innovations in the way things are done.

I then go on to describe as best I can the dynamics of the Innovation Maze. I close by outlining why this exercise can add considerable capacity to the top managers' group, in the form of members' supporting each other as the group struggles with problems of implementation.

Client (*another pause, a bit too long for my comfort level*): So you mean you are going to have us play games?

Consultant (*not surprised by this particular parry, because I have heard it many times before, yet slightly deflated regardless*): Not exactly, I don't think of these as games per se, but rather as group problem-solving exercises. They do not take a great deal of time and tie in well with what we would be trying to achieve together in this effort. I don't ask groups to participate in exercises that do not carefully fit organizational objectives jointly determined.

Client (*after yet another pause*): Well, I'm not sure. Several of us in the organization have done this sort of stuff before, and while it was fun, it really had little to do with what we were facing in the here-and-now, hard-nosed issues like downsizing, demands for high-performing systems and continuous quality improvement. Our problems are quite serious, and we were hoping to find someone who could help us get at them straightaway. After all, we don't have a lot of time we can dedicate to this endeavor. It's hard enough for us to carve out the any time at all, and I'm wary of anything that smacks of being touchy-feely.

Consultant (*heartbeat quickening*): I fully understand the constraints you're working under and the high expectations you have for this effort, and I will respect them throughout our work together. But I hope you can consider the possibility that improving group performance may require your stepping back from the exigencies you're facing and getting some purchase, some perspective so you can bore in again, this time more equipped to attack challenges differently. The only way I can help you do that is through some of these exercises, combined with the more traditional interactions we will have along the way—where I work directly with you and others on the tasks that need to get done.

Here I am tempted to go into much greater detail about the usefulness of the exercises for promoting reflection, the sometimes extraordinary power of metaphor to illuminate real-world problems, but I pull back, afraid of coming across as too theoretical.

At this point in the conversation, I know I have either created an opening or the door has shut, and I am just standing by waiting to sense it. In fact, at similar junctures in the past, I almost felt the whoosh of compressed air and heard the harsh clasp of metal on metal.

If she intends, even if unenthusiastically, to leave the door open, she will say, "Well, okay, let's get back to talking about what needs to be done and by when. How many months do you think it will take us to get to point A?" This is a good sign: Although skeptical, she feels there are enough offsetting advantages to proceed, albeit cautiously. More times than not, this intermediate outcome is the best I can hope for. If, however, she has chosen the latter path—more likely, in my experience—she will say, "Well, the approach sounds very interesting; let me think about it and get back to you." In other words, end of relationship. Goodbye.

Entry, Looking for Openings and Underpinnings

In this case, the relationship did not end. We moved ahead with the engagement. Before I discuss the dynamics of this next phase, a few words are in order about her and the organization she headed. She was a 20-year veteran of the agency, and for almost all that time had been on its small organizational development (OD) staff. OD had meant different things to each of the several agency heads she had served during her tenure in this 600-person organization. For one or two of them, she had been a strategic planning aide. Another had sought to use OD as an enforcer of policies developed at the top, policies to which all were supposed to adhere. Only one had understood that OD meant offering the staff of the agency opportunities to interpret the mission in ways that would increase their commitment and enthusiasm.

Recently, after a short stint as deputy director, or the agency's number-two person, she was asked to assume the mantle of leadership, the directorship. During her years in OD, she had held the idea that, given a shot at the top slot, she would help the agency align with a dramatically different policy context and work environment. She knew that times were changing, and quickly. Only a few years back, the agency had been the sole source of the services it provided. Now there were privately funded, even profit-inspired, entities on the scene seeking to provide similar services. In many instances these others were able to do this with less red tape, at lower cost, and with more of a smile to boot. Furthermore, the era of swelling employment rolls was over. Downsizing, or to be more politically correct, rightsizing, was now the order of the day, and it was taking hold with a vengeance.

Yet, the most compelling workplace challenge she faced grew out of changing attitudes and expectations on the part of staff. Fewer and fewer could tolerate the traditional chain of command that had operated for as long as the organization had been in existence. Though most of her top managers were still attached to a command-and-control model, even they could feel the winds of change.

There was, for example, the manifest yearning of the field office heads for more autonomy from the issuance of weekly orders from the central office. In fact, these 30 local-unit heads had gone so far as to establish their own informal association. It met regularly to address problems of common concern without any supervisors from the central office, that is, the division heads, in attendance.

Many of the newer staff, in support roles in the central office and customer service roles in the field offices, found the military model particularly anathema. They wanted support, a lot of it in fact, and there was increasing chatter among them about getting it from the community outside the agency rather than from the structure within it. Further, these staff had been acculturated in a workplace outfitted with all the tools that allowed one to work more independently. With access to a word processor, fax machine, cellular phone, and duplicating machine, a professional could do most things on the run, moving from place to place rather than being tethered to a fixed post in a single office setting.

As I looked at it, there were three ingredients in this engagement that drew my interest. First, it centered on organizational and personal transformation, so the obstacles would be significant and substantial; second, the sponsors seemed to understand that it would take a sustained period to achieve any results at all—18 months at least for initial payoff—so there were no illusions of quick fixes; and third, there were obvious connections in the effort to the larger problem of devolution of functions to more localized entities and even to private partners, so there was plenty of potential to learn about the challenges of decentralization, writ large.

When the agency head had called to say that she wished to engage my services, I said that I wanted the senior managers to have a shot at me and me at them before solidifying our arrangement. They were after all the main beneficiaries of the intervention. In short order, I was invited to an hour-long interview with two members of the senior managers' group and an OD aide. I explained to them, as I had to her, that much of what I would do in my work with them would not have them "sitting and gitting," or even, at first, groping together for solutions to the problems they faced. Rather, I would ask them to wrestle with the dynamics and implications of a set of experiences that I would present. Some would simulate problems all organizations face—group exercises or case studies, for example. Others would involve coming to terms with the real problems of the agency, including those of the senior managers, individually and collectively. Although I was unsure whether they understood the ramifications of the approach I was describing to them—or even the differences from more traditional approaches—they responded positively, and my engagement with them was confirmed.

My next move was to seek a meeting with the agency head to be sure that we had a common understanding of the engagement's aims and that she herself would be actively involved in it. I was quite satisfied with the outcomes of this meeting. She reconfirmed the view expressed by the small contingent I had just met with that the senior managers' group needed to shift its focus: from the management of day-to-day agency operations to the development of agency strategy; from "navel gazing," or attention to roles and relationships within the agency to "star gazing," or attention to relationships with other agencies and organizations; and from a preoccupation with managing the perceptions of those within the organization to a concern for managing the perceptions of those without, such as agency customers, political leaders, and the media.

She also gave me a commitment to full-scale involvement with the effort and direct and regular communication between the two of us. We agreed to get started with a letter of agreement between us that would include intended outcomes and the means of evaluating progress. We also acknowledged the need to feel our way into things rather than pretend we could forecast exact directions and dimensions at the outset. Given what was to happen before our 18 months were up, this caveat proved to be a wise one.

My first formal session with this new client took place at a regular meeting of the senior managers. Present were the agency head, the designated members of the senior management group, and two OD staffers. My aims for this session were to have them learn something about me, for me to learn something about them, and for them to learn something about each other. This last aim, their learning about each other, is a special concern of mine, especially in groups where many of the members have worked with each other for a long time. That they think they know all they need to know about each other is almost always worth putting to the test. If, in fact, they do learn new things about each other, these could become the building blocks for the establishment of new relationships.

In addition to the main aims, I also wanted to exemplify in this first session the potential advantages of experiential leadership development and to frame for them what this engagement would entail from my perspective. As it turned out, I was able to fulfill all these initial goals. Mapping Diversity and the Innovation Maze were both instrumental. The first brought a most positive end. To an extent that both startled and gratified me, the exercise brought to light information concerning the assets of individual members about which other members of the group had been in the dark.

Regarding the second, I had surmised beforehand that it would be particularly important in this first encounter not only to emphasize the need for senior managers to feel what it is like to risk innovation, but to do it in a way that fostered the kind of mutual support that is fundamental to team development. The Maze not only plants these notions solidly in participants' heads, it also lays down deep roots that sustain future growth. Nearly every time I have used the Maze, participants mull over its effects for a long period afterward, wrestling with the paradox that sometimes the best leadership develops from responsible and active followership.

Finally, a give-and-take between the group and me allowed me to present the major elements of the engagement as I saw them and allowed group members to provide their frank reactions. We also agreed that this initial interaction on what we would do together was a prelude to further contracting that would occur as our relationship unfolded.

The major surprise of this first meeting for me was the presence of a host of unresolved issues regarding group membership. Who exactly had a right to be in the room for the deliberations that would shape the role of the senior managers' group? This issue was broached early and directly when one person questioned the appropriateness of the OD staff being present. Others reinforced the point by wondering out loud if all the so-called senior managers really needed to be present, or just those with "line" responsibility, that is, those with big staffs and budgets.

Although I had not expected the issue of membership to emerge so quickly and so forthrightly, I was pleased that it had. The issue provided a fit segue to the round of individual interviews I had proposed as central to getting started on the effort. It also reinforced the need for getting to Working Norms as soon as possible. The norms could easily be fashioned to address issues of membership as well as more common concerns about members' interactions with each other in the course of their work together.

Endeavor, Skirting Success

Two main objectives governed my work with the senior managers' group over the ensuing months:

1. Help members move from their current approach to managing the agency—hands-on oversight of all operations—to strategic direction setting—heeding important central tendencies and providing needed support while ceding operational control to field-level managers. This meant that whatever we did together had to include plentiful opportunities for strategic thinking, general direction setting, and evaluation of outcomes—not talking about these things, but actually doing them. Then they would have ample material for reflection and analysis, and from these there could be real payoff in terms of learning and altered ways of operating.

2. Assist them in establishing effective working relationships with each other so that they could become a collective presence asserting clarity of agency mission and coordinated support of staff functions. There was plentiful evidence of the need for improvement in the quality of these relationships. The friction was palpable in my initial sessions with the senior managers. There were several references to old unclosed wounds, and as these were being voiced, most listeners maintained a tight-jawed reticence. It is axiomatic that even slight vestiges of disrespect or contention demonstrated in a meeting with an outsider can be multiplied many times over to reflect its real dimensions in normal agency routine.

The net goal of my aims was to help the senior managers shape themselves into an effective policy-setting and support unit. They had to become a group of mutually reinforcing leaders who could not only provide clearer direction for an agency buffeted by bureaucratic and political winds but also create required systems to help field staff better meet customer demands. The senior managers, with the aid and encouragement of their leader, needed to become a team.

Regrettably, team, as this book demonstrates, is one of the more loosely applied concepts in the contemporary organizational context. Properly used, it refers to a group of people brought together to accomplish specific goals. Together, they seek agreement on strategic options to be pursued, deliberate these options with rigor and respect, and make and hold to decisions as if they were one person. They then take well-coordinated action to fulfill their goals and send clear messages to all within the organization and outside about what they are doing. Most demanding of all, they hold each other accountable not only for results but for positive interactions along the way.

A group cannot become a team solely by studying the attributes of teamwork. A group has to do teamwork to become a team. It has to make mistakes, take time to reflect on and learn from them, and pick itself up and start again. Such fledgling teamwork is best done under the guidance of someone adept at helping group members learn from their experiences. The capacity for self-reflection is the fount from which effective teamwork springs. It is not part of our genetic endowment—it has to be learned and reinforced.

Thus, a group seeking to become a team needs to engage with the dynamics of teamwork, first in practice exercises but ultimately in a team project that offers reasonable prospects of success. By going through the paces of identifying a project, eliciting its challenges, and then taking them on, team members learn skills necessary for effective teamwork and can then apply them in their work context. Just as a group of middle managers brought together on a fishing pier in Maine can become a sailing crew by tackling appropriate tasks with support, so can senior managers become a strategic leadership team.

It is predictable therefore that after initial team-building exercises, I turned the attention of the senior managers to the identification and pursuit of a team project. Whatever common endeavor was chosen, it had to serve both as instructional device and as a tool for organizational development. More to the point, it had to present strategic challenges, that is, those with significant potential for long-term effect on the agency and its clients and ample opportunity for improving the senior managers' working relationships with each other.

After a few tense and awkward sessions, the project they chose was positioning the agency 5 years out, to achieve both smooth succession of staff leadership and equitable distribution of human and material resources. I acceded to this as the chosen common endeavor, but with considerable reluctance. Frankly, I thought the project too ambitious and that group members were not prepared yet to take on an effort of such magnitude. The project comprised too much the whole cloth of their job as strategic direction setters. It was not a more manageable chunk on which they might cut their teeth, feel success, and thereby build their capacity. After some back-and-forth on the matter, however, we agreed to proceed.

Three envisioned work products were to define the project's first phase. Each one was to be a plainly stated and succinct paper. Yet all would, as I had anticipated, be born of considerable struggle for common understanding among the senior managers and between the senior managers and their staffs.

The three products, as titled by the senior managers themselves were 1) "A Senior Manager's Code of Conduct," a 1-page document depicting the rules that would govern their deliberations with each other in light of their aspirations for a new role in the agency; 2) a short statement of agency underpinnings called "Positioning the Agency 5 Years Out," a 2-page document stating essential beliefs and commitments in regard to the agency's basic task and the larger context in which it was operating; and 3) a set of short strategy papers that would guide all in the agency as they formulated their annual business plans. Each strategy paper was to be only a few pages long. Topics included such matters as program delivery, human resource allocation, funding, and public information and advocacy.

For an outside consultant, the task of getting a group to produce paper products that fulfill stated objectives is not all that difficult. Getting a group to assume new responsibilities, such as strategic thinking and effective teamwork is very difficult, however. Papers can be composed and disposed. New tricks by old dogs require sustaining shifts in attitude and behavior. They not only require that individuals do their "A.M.s" and "P.M.s" differently. They also require the attainment of enough common understanding around the table so that members' actions are mutually consistent with each other and consonant with stated aims. Only when a level of common understanding is achieved can both staff and clients or customers experience the effects of agency decision making as more centering, more directed. Then, and only then, does the overall movement of the agency become more coordinated, efficient, and consequential.

So one key test of the success of a team development enterprise is the degree of common understanding that emerges within the group. This understanding makes for clearer messages, motivates concerted action, and lays the groundwork for more positive outcomes. Inspiring greater common understanding motivated most of my interactions with the senior managers, not only at the beginning of the effort but in the later stages as well. But common understanding about what?

First is common understanding about how members relate to each other as professionals and leaders. Second is common understanding of what the new role of the group is to be in the organization. Third is common understanding of how that new role should take shape in the form of a concrete demonstration.

After I had completed my initial contracting with senior managers, I set about interviewing each one in his or her office. What I learned from these interviews was that the 13 senior managers had among them nearly 200 years of combined service in the agency, an average of about 15 years per person. Such length of service was both a marked advantage and a signal disadvantage. Depth of background and experience in confronting difficult problems were offset by rutted behaviors and attitudes built around enduring wounds and encrusted stereotypes of colleagues. Long tenure for some also served as a shield from the potential contribution of the newer members of the group. The nearly two centuries of combined service made the achievement of common understanding on all fronts a significant challenge.

I also learned from the interviews that there were three distinct hierarchical subgroups within the senior management group. First were the line division heads, those who oversaw the field units. These four were the elite, excepting the director, who had singular lead status. Second were the division heads who ran central office support units. The four of them were the struggling subelite. Last were the staff heads of key functions such as budget and public information. These four were seen by their colleagues as relative interlopers in the group. They were the "others." The existence of such a strong pecking order could easily prevent the emergence of an equal voice for all around the table. Because equal voice is a *sine qua non* of common understanding, achieving it was going to be tricky.

Early on in our work together, I had asked the senior managers to do Towering Vision and Feedback Theater. My purposes were to foster greater cohesion around agency direction and at the same time to have the group experience the inherently awkward connection between planning and implementation in an organization. Planning has much greater status than implementation, and those who do planning usually see themselves as superior to those who implement. Yet implementation is the field where the seeds of planning are sown. There can be no harvest without it.

Simple as it may sound, I needed the senior managers to know in their bodies and minds how the policy intent of those at the top is often poorly communicated to those with the responsibility for implementing it. Even when communication from on high is crisp and clear, intent and content are often misconstrued by staff. In fact, those whose main job is day-to-day interaction with clients frequently resent even wise and rational policy that is well communicated, simply because they have played little part in its development.

If strategic policy direction was to be their role, the senior managers had to be more prepared for the communication problems they would encounter as they formulated policies for the rest of the organization to implement. When, for example, the senior managers and I discussed how to unveil the draft "Positioning" document for the benefit of the field office heads, the lessons of Towering Vision and Feedback Theater stared them in the face. They offered useful guidance on how to avoid confounding an important invitation, leaving the invitees, that is, staff, feeling confused and resentful rather than included and essential. In fact, the group and I were able to develop a strategy for involving the field office heads in the revision and refinement of the draft in a way that minimized the latter's rejection of it as "foreign tissue" and maximized the potential for a graft that had a chance of actually taking.

I also used Bureaucracy at this juncture to reinforce and build on the lessons gleaned from Towering Vision and Feedback Theater. Bureaucracy served as an effective means of increasing the senior managers' understanding of the hard work they would have to do to overcome the debilitating effects of the hierarchical relationships they had with each other and with staff. The three strata they had established in their own ranks and the rigid layering that gripped the whole organization stood squarely in the way of solid agencywide teamwork. The reactions of several individuals were gut level and hard to overcome. At stake was status both inside and outside the group, and those with the most status found it very difficult to let go of it. Even after selected exercises like those just noted and several sessions that focused on this issue, internal memos addressed as follows would still pop up: to "senior managers," with copies (cc) to four people who were themselves senior managers. Membership issues all over again! They persisted throughout the engagement—sometimes they abated, but they were always present.

Despite shortfalls like these, some of the initial aims of this leadership development effort were beginning to be fulfilled. After 6 months of intense sessions that alternated between experiential exercises and focused deliberations, a senior managers' code of conduct was in place. Working Norms, Discussion Functions, and Marking Team Leadership had played a significant role in assisting with this. Laminated versions of the code of conduct, wall sized and wallet sized, had been distributed to all the senior managers. A few of the larger ones also appeared on walls throughout the office, and some of the smaller ones found their way into the hands of other staff, including field office staff. Selected senior managers had invoked the code more than once in their meetings, especially to remind colleagues that they were supposed to behave in mutually respectful ways.

There was a credible draft of a "Positioning" statement, and the senior managers had begun to develop a plan to gain others' understanding and ownership of it. Although the language in the draft was still vague, it did approach, if not completely address, matters of equity and succession. Four rough-draft strategy papers had been circulated for comment by all in the agency.

Ending, All Too Soon

At this point in the engagement—about 8 months in—an event of enormous consequence occurred. A far-reaching early retirement option was announced. It offered an attractive financial package to about one third of the agency's staff. If all who were eligible did in fact take advantage of it, one third of the senior management group would depart, several key central office functions would be gutted, and the staffing of more than one field office would be zeroed out.

The organization quickly went into a tailspin. Concern over organizational self-actualization in a new age evaporated. On almost everybody's part there was nearly an instantaneous reversion to a preoccupation with survival. In one day, Maslow's hierarchy of needs was turned upside down. Given what was happening, the senior managers' project on succession seemed especially ironic. A powerful force from the outside had just overturned the possibility of organized and rational succession of key staff from within.

One of those who could exercise an option for retirement was the agency head herself. She and all the rest of the senior managers, individually and collectively, drew inward. Whether intending to retire, uncertain about doing so, or sure to remain, senior managers to a person seemed dazed by the fast-forward flux that had ensnared them. Within a week of this major new development, they asked to meet with me and suggested we close on our mutual arrangement because "most of the objectives had been fulfilled." They asserted that they had improved their teamwork, and the draft positioning and strategy statements were being circulated for comment within the agency. To paraphrase, "Let's declare victory and withdraw."

My work with the agency was put on hold. The agency head herself expressed the need to finalize her own plans and assess their effect on others before proceeding. She also wanted to see which senior managers would take the retirement option. She asserted that the intervention effort could then resume in the context of clarity about her fate, as well as the composition and constitution of what would inevitably be a smaller senior management group.

In the 2 months that followed, much happened. The agency head decided to take early retirement herself, as did 4 of the 13 senior managers. Two others left the agency for other posts. This left a total of seven senior managers. The actual number of retirees in the agency as a whole was 200, or slightly less than one third of the agency's total staff complement.

During this 2 months' hiatus, the director concentrated on restructuring the new agency to adapt to the inevitable downsizing it was about to endure. Although one could have made a convincing argument about their usefulness in these extreme circumstances, consultant services were readily sacrificed. I had one updating session with the agency head, but the engagement was not revived.

Implications

From this story, one can distill truths that have to be reckoned with if leadership development is to increase its influence on organizational functioning.

Leadership Development Depends on Effective Connections

Such connections are hard to come by through traditional means, and less traditional means, although promising, remain unperfected. In the joint effort just described, I wanted to effect a whole series of connections, all of which were tenuous. First were the connections I asked the client to make at the point of initial discussions about our working together. I wanted the client to risk using a brand of leadership development that deviated from traditional approaches. Next were the connections I attempted to foster between myself and the top leadership of the organization, the agency head and the senior managers. These were meant to be the foundation for our work together, the bases on which that work could proceed toward fulfillment. In the endeavor itself were the connections I encouraged on the part of the senior managers. These were supposed to be the most consequential of all. Experiential exercises, the formulation and execution of a senior managers' project, guided reflection, and facilitated give-and-take were all designed to engender and solidify in the senior managers' minds a new definition of their collective leadership role in the organization.

That any of these connections were made and maintained defies the odds. The skepticism of many clients about the paltry learning potential in experiential exercises is understandable. Expressions such as *icebreakers, playing games, touchy-feely stuff,* and *bonding experience* capture the standard reaction, a combination of dismissal and cynicism, a sense that if there are effects, they are about as deep and enduring as those offered by mild entertainment. The judgment seems to be that the experiences share little connection with serious endeavor, in that they do not affect the way people think about or do serious work in organizations.

This asserted lack of connection has two causes, both of which are remediable. At present, most facilitators fail to orchestrate connections between what unfolds in an experiential exercise and the real demands on people in organizations. If these connections are made at all, they are superficial and ephemeral, rarely elaborated and dwelt on so that participants can invest critical thought in them, speculate on potential applications, and then actually do things differently. Second, the experiences are rarely connected to the natural penchant of participants to engage in concept formation about organizational functioning. Whatever their formal job assignments, all denizens of organizations are amateur organizational development specialists. Not taking advantage of either of these opportunities means that experiential exercises are often left in the form of pure potential, rarely actualized in terms of the way people think about organizations and work in them. This diminishes the odds of fit connections and the potential for positive effect.

What Seems to Be an Indirect Path and a Slow Pace May in Fact Lead Most Directly and Readily to Desired Results

There is a powerful and abiding misconception at work in the world of organizations today: The route to successful completion of important tasks is a straight line followed with as much effort and dispatch as possible. Most organizational leaders believe, it appears, that the way to develop good strategy is to put the brightest and most influential staff in a room together and have them, either by themselves or with the help of outside experts, talk hard and fast about strategic planning. These are the people, after all, who know the necessary ingredients of good strategy; many have done this kind of work before; and they are capable individuals who can overcome most challenges in front of them if they just press on. Right?

Wrong! The straight-line approach is in almost all instances a recipe for a mediocre outcomes on an assignment that has in it the seeds of significant change in the way the organization interacts with its external environment and its staff. If, for example, the group members are familiar with each other, all the patterns that have stood in the way of their fulfilling important aims in the past will continue to stand in the way. In fact, as they "get down to work" on this new task, the sheer magnitude of it and the underlying uncertainties that attend it will call into play some of the most retrogressive tendencies that inhere in the group. Inevitably, these will pull it down and hold it back.

If the group members are new to each other, the stumbling blocks will be of different dimension, but no less inhibiting. The group will have developed no agreed-on rules of engagement, and therefore will not be able to marshal collective capacity for generating creative ideas and approaches. In all likelihood, the group will move speedily down the road of formulation, only to find itself backtracking a week later, groping for basic understanding on how to listen to each other and build on other's ideas.

In effect, either because of past familiarity or the lack of it, the quality of group work often suffers if essential groundwork is overlooked. Members will be into the task and will have done nothing to enhance individual and collective capabilities, nothing to see things differently from the way they did before, nothing to create a foundation for effective interaction. Until they can gain some experience in common that promotes these, they will vainly be seeking higher quality and blithely assuming they can achieve it with capacities that are best characterized by the expression "the same old, same old."

Embracing Dynamic Tensions
Yields Positive Results

Real productivity in the client-consultant relationship derives from a pull and tug between the two. The only right reason to seek an organizational consultant, or to be one, is an impulse toward changes that will make things better. One does not need a high-priced consultant to keep things as they are, unless political blessings are the sole aim—which unfortunately in all too many instances is the case.

It is axiomatic that needed change is bred of and breeds tensions within and between all players. There is tension to begin with in the mind of the client who, by seeking outside assistance, is expressing discomfort with the status quo. This tension is mirrored in the mind of the consultant who, if worth any salt, has well-held views about how things might be improved. Finally, there is inevitably tension between the two because of the different positions they occupy with regard to the situation at hand—invested insider against unbiased outsider.

This clash of perspectives frequently finds its way into the very first interchange between the insider and the outsider. Regardless of how compatible their views and personalities are, it normally persists throughout their relationship. This was certainly the case in the story just told. The coming together of client and consultant was uneven. Although they managed to work their way into a similar mindset, they stumbled at the crux point. Change, instead of being accelerated, was forestalled.

Assessing the nature of the tensions that abide at any given time and deciding whether they are likely to create benefits rather than detriments requires great presence of mind. Can the client, for example, see that what is on the face of a problem may be different from some more consequential underlying frames? Can the consultant absorb a sense of the exigencies the client feels and adjust his or her approach accordingly, without diluting its effect? If the door remains open between the two, can they press ahead together, thus enhancing the possibility of significant benefit for the organization? That there is tension is good. Whether there can also be growth in the relationship and positive yield from it is the key question. The only thing that can be said with confidence is that the absence of tension almost always means that the consulting arrangement sought is a reinforcement of the status quo rather than an attempt to move away from it.

Those committed to organizational improvement should seek these truths.

Effective Connections, the Indirect Path, Embracing Tensions

If, as a consultant, I cannot convince a client to try something different, something that may feel like a step back at first, a set of experiences whose connections to their most substantive concerns is at the outset a bit hazy, then I normally forego the engagement. By the close of an

initial conversation it is clear whether the client's focus on the fulfillment of an impulse toward change is an opening to a wider vista or
merely a case of tunnel vision that will prevent much movement. It is
also clear that the courage to persist receives its greatest test at the crux
point of a change effort, in the middle of the endeavor when all the
groundwork has been done and the threshold is ready to be crossed.
Whether it will be crossed is the ultimate litmus test for organizational
change.

CHAPTER 8

Conclusion

Let me redraw the path this book traverses. It begins with an interaction on a dock and ends with applications in an agency. In between these are reflections on the state-of-the-art of leadership development and demonstrations of how to use relatively low-cost forms of experiential leadership development to improve group performance in organizations.

The progression is from a narrow frame—face-to-face leader-group interchange—to a wide view—the broad leadership development landscape and the theoretical backdrop behind my own personal philosophy of teaching leadership. This is followed by another shift, from the wide view to the ground level—the area beneath one's feet—in the form of 25 different ways of bringing ideas about experiential leadership development to life. When deployed strategically—used in appropriate combinations and sequences—and debriefed artfully, the exercises can significantly enhance the fulfillment of important organizational goals.

Interactions

From the brief interaction captured in the Prologue, the book expands into a much more encompassing set of interactions between the reader and me as commentator, and between the reader and the experiences contained in the exercises, both the activity and the debrief. The aim of all the interactions is to place leadership development in what I believe is its most appropriate context, teaching and learning.

The inspiration for all these interactions is the legendary story of Mark Hopkins on the log. Hopkins, a 19th-century American archetype, was noted for his unusual approach to teaching. He positioned himself on one end of a fallen log, with a student on the other, and then engaged in a vigorous dialogue with his companion. The ensuing back-and-forth inevitably became as rich-grained as the log on which they sat.

Reflections

Chapter 1, "Ways of Thinking About Leadership Development," serves as a review of the current literature on leadership development and an exposition of my own thinking about teaching leadership. It arrives, as I did after two decades, at a place of marked promise, still not fully explored and certainly not fully exploited—experiential approaches to teaching team leadership—so as to meet major organizational challenges, such as risking innovation, building teams, managing conflict, and using diversity.

Demonstrations

The 25 exercises are the principal demonstration vehicles. They are introduced by a set of general pointers on how to set up, conduct, and discuss them; and they are organized by the primary leadership development objective they fulfill. For each of the 25, there is a set of explicit directions, thoughts on strategic deployment and successful application, and an array of proposed questions that point the way to successful postexercise discussions with participants.

Applications

Interactions, reflections, and demonstrations serve important ends. Chapter 7, "The Exercises in Play," is an extended story that dwells on the effects of the approach advocated in this book. It is intended to show how experiential leadership development can be woven into the fabric of an actual undertaking designed to improve the functioning of a large service organization. The story not only conveys some of the promise of the approach outlined in prior chapters. It also reflects the fragility of all organizational development efforts, regardless of approach.

Interaction, reflection, demonstration, and application—these make up a framework for the specialized material presented in this book. Interestingly, they also provide a useful structure for thinking about the field of leadership and organizational development in general. Reflect yourself on the value of the sequence. First, inquire about the signal human interactions that deserve attention. Then, take a step back from them and reflect not only on what is being done in the field, but what should be done according to one's best lights. Next, demonstrate in clear and concrete ways a desirable approach. Finally, delineate its applications to leadership and organizational development broadly construed.

References

Argyris, C. (1992). *On organizational learning*. Boston: Blackwell Business.

Bohm, D. (1990). *Dialogue: An introduction*. Pamphlet.

Bolman, L. & Deal, T. (1991). *Reframing organizations: Artistry, choice, and leadership*. San Francisco: Jossey-Bass.

Bolman, L., & Deal, T. (1994). Looking for leadership: Another search party's report. *Educational Administration Quarterly, 30*(1), 77-96.

Brown, M. (1990). The bone game: A ritual of transformation. *Journal of Experiential Education, 13*(1), 48-52.

Burke, W. W. (1997). The new agenda for organizational development. *Organizational Dynamics, 26*(1), 7-20.

Clarke, K., & Clarke, M. (1994). *Choosing to lead*. Charlotte, NC: Center for Creative Leadership.

Cohen, E., & Tichy, N. (1997). How leaders develop leaders. *Training and Development, 51*(5), 58-74.

Conger, J. (1993). The brave new world of leadership training. *Organizational Dynamics, 21*(3), 46-58.

Csoka, L. S. (1996). The rush to leadership training. *Across the Board, 33*(8), 28-32.

Dewey, J., (1938). *Education and experience*. New York: Collier.

Drucker Foundation. (1996). *The leader of the future*. San Francisco: Jossey-Bass.

Drucker, P. (1974). *Management: Tasks, practices, responsibilities.* New York: Harper & Row.

Gardner, H. (1995). *Leading minds: An anatomy of leadership.* New York: Basic Books.

Heifitz, R. (1994). *Leadership without easy answers.* Cambridge, MA: Harvard University Press.

Kaagan, S. (1997). *Leadership lessons: From a life of character and purpose in public affairs.* Lanham, MD: University Press of America.

Kaagan, S., & Donahue, W. (1996, April). *Collaborative Leadership Capacities Inventory.* Developed for the Life Communicators' Association Leadership Development Conference, East Lansing, MI.

Katzenbach, J., & Smith, D.(1993). The discipline of teams. *Harvard Business Review, 71*(2), 111-124.

Keys, J. B. (1988). Management education and development: Current issues and emerging trends. *Journal of Management, 14*(2), 205-229.

Keys, J. B. (Ed). (1990). Management games and simulations [Special issue]. *Journal of Management Development, 9*(2).

Kouzes, J. M., & Posner, B. Z. (1991). *The leadership challenge: How to get extraordinary things done in organizations.* San Francisco: Jossey-Bass.

Newhauser, J. J. (1976). Business games have failed. *Academy of Management Review, 1*(4), 124-129.

O'Toole, J. (1995). *Leading change: The argument for values-based leadership.* New York: Ballantine.

Proudman, S., (1992). Experiential education as emotionally-engaged learning. *Journal of Experiential Education, 15*(2), 19-23.

Raelin, J. (1997). Action learning and action science: Are they different? *Organizational Dynamics, 26*(1), 21-34.

Rohnke, K. (1984). *Silver bullets: A guide to initiative problems, adventure games, and trust activities.* Dubuque, IA: Kendall/Hunt.

Schon, D. (1983). *The reflective practitioner: How professionals think in action.* New York: Basic Books.

Senge, P. (1990). *The fifth discipline.* Garden City, NY: Doubleday.

Stumpf, S. A., & Dutton, J. E. (1990). The dynamics of learning through management simulations: Let's dance. *Journal of Management Development, 9*(2), 7-15.

Terry, R., (1993). *Authentic leadership: Courage in action.* San Francisco: Jossey-Bass.

Vicere, A. (1996). Executive education: The leading edge. *Organizational Dynamics, 25*(2), 67-82.

Wells, R. A. (1990). Management games and simulations in management development: An introduction. *Journal of Management Development, 9*(2), 4-6.

About the Author

Stephen S. Kaagan has served since 1991 as Professor in the College of Education at Michigan State University. Previously, he was a chief state education officer (Vermont Education Commissioner), academic head of a higher education institution (Provost, Pratt Institute), and chief executive of a nonprofit educational organization (President, Hurricane Island Outward Bound). He has been a classroom teacher and has taught organization development and educational policy at Pratt Institute, Rutgers University, and the University of Southern Maine. He has a master's and a doctorate from Harvard University and a bachelor's from Williams College, as well as honorary doctorates from Williams College and Green Mountain College. He has consulted on team leadership development, strategic planning, and organization development with an array of government, business, and nonprofit organizations, and has written extensively on leadership, accountability of public organizations, and the role of the arts in education.